THE TWELVE RULES FOR
STRAIGHT THINKING

THE TWELVE RULES FOR STRAIGHT THINKING

Applied to Business and Personal Problems

by

WILLIAM J. REILLY, Ph.D.

BUSINESS CONSULTANT

FOUNDER AND DIRECTOR,

NATIONAL INSTITUTE FOR STRAIGHT THINKING

HARPER & BROTHERS

NEW YORK AND LONDON

Portions of the material found in this book were originally
published by Harper & Brothers in *Straight Thinking*, 1935,
and *How to Use Your Head*, 1938.

TABLE OF CONTENTS

CONTENTS

Reilly's twelve rules for straight thinking have been widely used and acclaimed by students, members, and clients of the National Institute for Straight Thinking, and by many readers of his earlier books on this important subject.

Ever since Dr. Reilly wrote his doctor's dissertation under my direction at The University of Chicago some twenty years ago, I have followed his work with much interest and pride, and it did not surprise me when I learned that he had succeeded in reducing the elusive human thought process to a few simple rules which any layman can understand and use.

Soon after he received his basic training, first as an engineering student, and then as a member of the research staff, at Carnegie Institute of Technology, Dr. Reilly began to apply the methods of the pure sciences in his search for the underlying laws and principles which govern the thinking, the habits, and the behavior of man.

In 1928, he defined the law of retail gravitation, which explains how consumer buying habits of people in smaller cities and towns are influenced by the proximity of a larger city.

In 1929, he worked out a simple miniature-sample method for testing the accuracy and reliability of market information.

In 1938, he charted the path of the one-track mind and its relation to orderly thinking.

In 1942, he charted the four primary mental levels in all human relations and showed how we can open closed minds with a simple mental attitude which conforms with all the fundamental rules for straight thinking.

In 1945, he defined the law of intelligent action which represents a significant and far-reaching contribution to our knowledge of people and what makes them act as they do.

When Dr. Reilly first announced the twelve rules for straight thinking in 1933, I had the pleasure of contributing to the first seminar group for the purpose of working out practical applications of the rules, and I am persuaded that their continued application in the fields of business and education will become increasingly important as the years go by.

NATHANIEL WARING BARNES
Executive Secretary,
Association of Consulting
Management Engineers, Inc.

The purpose of this book is to present the Twelve Rules for Straight Thinking, and to show how they can be used to solve a wide variety of business, educational, personal, and social problems. It will be of interest to business men, educators, parents, students, or to anyone else who has a sincere desire to improve his thinking or the thinking of others.

The development of these rules has an interesting background. In 1922, when I was a member of the research staff at Carnegie Institute of Technology, I observed the care and precision with which students in the scientific laboratory followed a certain approved procedure—how they tested their observations, defined their problems, gathered their experimental evidence, and arrived at properly qualified conclusions.

But I also noticed that when these same students stepped across the hall from the scientific laboratory to the study of human problems, in economics, or business, or psychology, they carried little of their orderly procedure with them, and seemed bewildered as to just how such human problems should be handled.

Intrigued by this obvious contradiction, I began some early attempts to adapt the organized thinking employed in the scientific laboratory to our every-day human problems.

Later, while on the research staff at The University of Chicago, and at The University of Texas, I engaged in a comprehensive search of the literature on logic. This search revealed that while orderly procedures had been followed for years in the pure sciences, apparently no one had ever defined specifically the mental process of straight thinking in the social sciences; no comprehensive rules had been set down to help the student to think straight on problems which involved human behavior.

I then visited leading colleges and universities where I interviewed outstanding educational leaders on the subject of straight thinking. In these consultations with logicians, psychologists, and social scientists, the orderly procedure followed in the scientific laboratory was used as the basis for the development of simple rules that could be applied safely to problems involving human behavior. Finally, twelve simple rules were defined and agreed upon. Here, for the first time, straight thinking was expressed in non-technical, easily understood form, which any normal person can use to think for himself.

In the Fall of 1932, the National Institute for Straight Thinking was founded for the purpose of applying the rules for straight thinking to business and career problems. Since that time, the rules have been successfully applied to a wide variety of other problems as well.

PREFACE

Grateful acknowledgment is hereby given to the late Professor George H. Follows who invited me to initiate these studies at Carnegie Institute of Technology; to Dr. Walter F. Rittman, who collaborated with me on my first study of "What Becomes of the Carnegie Institute of Technology Engineering Graduate?" and who encouraged me to extend these early researches further; to Mr. N. W. Barnes, who directed my doctor's dissertation at The University of Chicago; to Mr. Arthur H. Hert, who acted as my research assistant at The University of Texas; to Dr. W. W. Charters, Director, Bureau of Educational Research, Ohio State University, who was the first to suggest that I take my case materials on common mistakes in thinking and use them as a basis for the development of positive rules; to Professor James C. Boudreau, Director of the School of Fine and Applied Arts, Pratt Institute, who sponsored my experimental work with members of the senior class there; to the many business and industrial clients whose organizations served as proving grounds for the practical application of the rules for straight thinking; and finally, to members and alumni of the National Institute for Straight Thinking, far too numerous to mention, who contributed much of the factual case material upon which this book is based.

Portions of the material found in this book were originally published by Harper & Brothers in two earlier books: "Straight Thinking," 1935, and "How to Use

Your Head," 1938. These two earlier books have been combined, revised, and brought up-to-date, and are here presented in one authoritative volume.

The presentation of the material in this book has been greatly clarified by the continued editorial criticism given by Gladys Bogue Reilly.

W. J. R.

January, 1947

CHAPTER ONE

Introduction

NO MATTER WHERE YOU GO, YOU CAN ARRIVE AT A common agreement with almost any thoughtful person that what the world needs is more straight thinking.

Educators agree that the primary purpose of general education is to "induce people to think . . . to think straight if possible . . . to think always for themselves." Business men agree that any successful executive must be able to think his way through the various problems which arise day in and day out, and he must enjoy a good batting average in arriving at the right decision or the best course of action to be followed.

In fact, in every business, art, trade, or profession, we know that crooked thinking costs money and leads to failure. We know that, in our social life, it costs us our self-respect and the friendship and admiration of others.

We know that crooked thinking may cause us to marry the wrong person or to continue to work at some job for which we are not fitted and which we do not enjoy.

We know that crooked thinking permits politicians to stampede us into voting for the wrong person. It enables "clever" lawyers to trick us into bringing in the wrong verdict.

We know that crooked thinking causes us to pay disgracefully low salaries to those in charge of the important task of educating our children.

We know that crooked thinking causes personal jealousies, family arguments, neighborhood quarrels, business feuds, political hatreds, religious intolerance, international disputes, WARS.

We know that crooked thinking makes us nervous, gives us a sour stomach, leads to overwork, then to a mental breakdown, and in some extreme cases, to insanity which may be defined as unbalanced and crooked thinking.

Straight thinking has never been responsible for any of these ills.

Straight thinking is the greatest insurance against them.

In short, we know that there are a lot of things wrong with our thinking. And we want to correct it. The whole trouble is that no one has ever given us a simple plan for straightening it out. Until recently, we have not known the answer to the question, "What is straight thinking and how do you do it?"

This is not surprising.

When you consider the fact that it took man about 99 million years, more or less, to learn to walk on his hind legs; that as recently as a half million years ago he was wandering around living in caves; that less than 500 years ago, Columbus was considered crazy because he said the world was not flat; that less than 400 years ago, Galileo was imprisoned because he said the world was not the center of the universe, but that it traveled around the sun; that only 70 years ago when Mr. Bell first showed the "speaking telephone" to New York, there were plenty of doubters who just didn't believe that a voice could travel all the way across the river from Brooklyn on a copper wire; and that even more recently than that, Westinghouse was considered a little balmy when he seriously proposed stopping a train with "wind";—when we consider all this, we begin to realize that after all, this fellow called MAN is a guy who acted like an ape for quite a stretch, and that this business of acting like a gentleman is still a comparatively new idea with him. He's bought himself some nice clothes and covered himself with a thin veneer of "civilization." He has already made some interesting beginnings in applying orderly thinking to material things outside himself, he has made some big firecrackers with which he can destroy himself, but he is just now getting around to the business of exploring the operation of the one little organ inside his head that dictates everything he does.

Most of our so-called thinking has become so automatic that we are not in the least aware of what is really happening in our brain. If we stop to consider what we are doing, however, we can see that our whole life presents a perpetual stream of problems, each of which *demands* a decision. Every day we make a number of decisions on business and on personal matters, whether we realize it or not. At the end of a week we have made hundreds of decisions.

We arrive at many of our decisions by taking a hop, skip, and a jump from an observation to a conclusion without employing any reasoning whatsoever.

Some of our decisions are governed by prejudices or emotions that happen to sway us at the moment. Some of them are made by default—that is, by "letting things go."

There are many disagreeable decisions that we like to postpone. But when we postpone a decision we *really make one.*

When you put off a trip to the dentist, it is the same as if you decided to let the tooth get worse. The man with a toothache would say you were crazy if you told him that he had actually decided to have that toothache. But that is exactly what he did when he postponed his trip to the dentist. And none of my relatives are dentists.

Or if you postpone a decision to cut the expenses of a business, it is the same as if you decided to let the expenses remain as they are.

The real question, then, is not whether you need to make decisions or not, for YOU DO. The real question is:

4

INTRODUCTION

"Will your decisions be based on straight thinking or not? Will your decisions be logical and sound or will they be governed by 'hit or miss' thinking, saturated with prejudice and emotion, or arrived at by default?"

Two simple questions confront anyone who is interested in straight thinking:

1. What are the *negative* tendencies—the faulty mental attitudes and common mistakes—that keep me from thinking straight, and how can I learn to avoid them? (This is what the social scientist calls a difficulty analysis.)
2. What are the *positive* rules for straight thinking and how can I learn to use them? (This is commonly called a job analysis.)

Chapter Two, therefore, will be devoted to a brief identification of some of the more important faulty mental attitudes and common mistakes that frustrate orderly thinking, so that they may be easily recognized and avoided. Following chapters will deal in more detail with the positive rules for straight thinking. You will find these twelve rules simple to understand and simple to use.

Why We Don't Think Straight

IT IS NATURAL FOR US TO TAKE FOR GRANTED OUR OWN ability to think straight. We would like to believe, and for the most part do believe, that we are fair and open-minded. Although we can often see that the conclusions of another person are false, extravagant, prejudiced, or one-sided, each of us is inclined to feel that his own thinking is quite reasonable.

Anyone, however, who will take the time and exercise the patience necessary to review and to analyze his own thought processes, as well as those of his friends, will probably conclude that the everyday thinking of most of us is not very orderly and not very sound.

Faulty Mental Attitudes

The common mistakes in thinking that we make day in and day out can all be traced back to faulty mental attitudes. So, before we discuss these common mistakes, let us first explore the faulty mental attitudes that are responsible for them.

6

"FER IT" OR "AGIN IT"?

In order to illustrate one important tendency in the thinking of all of us in such a way that it will be brought home in a hurry, let's try a little experiment. Consider the following question for four or five minutes without reading further.

"Do you think we should share the secrets of the atomic bomb and all other instruments of warfare with other nations all over the world?"

Now stop. Don't read on until you have thought this question over for a few minutes at least.

What is your answer? Isn't it true that you are taking sides on this question? Isn't it true that you are either "fer it" or "agin it," without really knowing a whole lot about it? Isn't it true that you are harboring in your mind a conviction to which you are not entitled —a conviction which would handicap your impartial study of that question?

Just how much do you know about the so-called atomic bomb secrets? It is generally recognized that scientists scattered all over the world know how to split the atom. Of course, there is considerable talk about our atomic bomb production "know how." But here again, even the most optimistic agree that this is only a temporary advantage.

The important point is that no one has any well-rounded facts concerning the wisdom of sharing the secrets of the atomic bomb and all other instruments of warfare with other nations all over the world. It has never been tried. Meanwhile, no one is entitled to be either "fer it" or "agin it." Yet nearly everyone you talk with has a firm conviction.

Try another question:

"Do you think a college education helps a young man in business?"

You will probably find yourself prejudiced on either one side or the other of this question, too. This general question would be rejected by the seasoned thinker, who would ask, "What kind of college education, for what kind of young man entering what kind of business, and where?"

If you doubt that it is generally true that we start out by taking sides on all sorts of general and incomplete questions, try throwing controversial questions of this kind up in the air for discussion the next time you are in the company of a group of people. You will find that, no matter what question you suggest, practically everyone in the group will be either "fer it" or "agin it."

In almost every business conference there is a certain order in which men usually express themselves on any subject—usually in order of the authority of their position. The top men have their say first.

Now here's George, an assistant manager of some department or other, seated down toward the end of the table. The "gassing" has been going on for thirty or forty minutes, and George's mind has started to wander. He may be thinking of last night when he was playing with his little boy in the front room, and barked his shin. "Gosh! that thing is beginning to hurt a little," he says to himself as he casually adjusts his garter with one hand under the table. "Huh! right under the garter."

Just then the leader of the meeting says, "What do *you* think of this, George?"

George's ears fly up as he shakes himself out of the trance.

"Why—well, I'll tell you, Mr. Johnson, I don't like the color of it. It is too yellow. Frankly, it—it doesn't look right to me."

Now the damage has been done! George has committed himself to an opinion. From that moment on, therefore, he begins to spend the company's time and money in an opportunistic pursuit of any or all kinds of evidence that will support the wisdom of this half-baked opinion which he has expressed on the spur of the moment.

This costs money in business. In fact, business is full of feuds and disagreements arising from such ill-considered opinions.

How easy and how foolish it is to go off half-cocked and express a hunch or an opinion under the pressure of a question from some one else. Once we express ourselves, though, we are inclined to stick to that position, even though we later have the sneaking feeling in the seat of our pants that we were wrong about the whole thing. Yes, we stick to it. We stick to it in spite of hell or high water. And sometimes we suffer the anguish of hell because of it. And sometimes the high water comes and drowns us out of our job. Such cases are common. Who hasn't observed that once we express an opinion— be it ever so false—we tend to be ever so true to it?

WE DON'T KNOW SPECIFICALLY
WHAT WE ARE TALKING ABOUT

Nearly every morning the elevator operator asks me, "How's things?"

"Going pretty good," is my usual reply.

That, with minor variations, is generally the substance of our conversations.

Neither of us is talking about anything specifically; neither of us knows what the other is talking about; or, for that matter, what he himself is talking about.

My conversations with the elevator man have the same earmarks as so many everyday business conversations. Some months ago I walked into the club car of New York Central's crack train—the Twentieth Century Limited—speeding west. There I found three business men engaged in a heated argument over business conditions.

One said that business had "turned the corner"— was "on the up and up."

The second argued that business was getting "worse and worse"—"going to the dogs."

The third held that business had finally reached its "normal equilibrium" and "would continue along the present sane level for some time to come."

It was not until a fourth man interrupted the loud talking with a few questions concerning just exactly what the gladiators were arguing about, that it came to light that each was really talking about his own business; that one was in the shoe business in Boston, the second was in the real estate business in Chicago, and the third was in the candy business in Schenectady, and that none of them knew a whole lot about business in general.

So many business arguments are like that. In the first place, we seldom define exactly what we are talking about. In the second place, we argue on subjects that we don't know much about. We make the observation that business is good or bad without stating specifically, or even *thinking* specifically, what kinds of business, in what geographical locations, among what types of customers we refer to, and without defining exactly what we mean by "good" or "bad."

We worship words whose meanings we have never explored. We may boast that we are "conservative" without being aware that the word means "opposed to change" and without considering that no progress can be made without favorable change.

Don't get me wrong. I don't mean to say that we have to know what we are talking about in order to carry on an enjoyable conversation. Conversation does not have to have any point to it if the purpose is to while away the time and enjoy ourselves. "Conversation" is considered to be a lost art by many who feel that the ultimate achievement in the art is the facility to talk for hours about nothing at all.

Personally, however, I have never felt that knowing what you are talking about and having a point to your conversation, takes any of the enjoyment out of it or detracts very much from the art.

OUR THOUGHTS REVOLVE ABOUT OURSELVES

It is not so difficult to be sane and reasonable when we are dealing with matters that involve other people's affairs. But as soon as our own interests become involved, our thoughts begin to revolve about ourselves, our thinking becomes influenced by varying degrees of emotion, our point of view becomes egocentric.

We are prejudiced against any ideas that interfere with our personal pride or possessions. Right now it is difficult for you to accept the idea that you are not fair-minded, not logical, not reasonable, simply because your pride is involved. Then, concerning your possessions, you admit only with reluctance that something you bought is not worth what you paid for it.

A mother enjoys the belief that her children are far more attractive or talented than her neighbor's or her friend's.

"My product is the best in the world," screams Mr. Manufacturer in a full-page ad. "Sez you," is the comeback of all competitors and many consumers.

Most of us reason as if all the world were like ourselves. A manufacturer's concept of his market so often revolves about his own individual experiences, likes, and dislikes. How often have you heard an advertising or sales executive, in talking about "the consumer market," mention his wife to illustrate a point—as if she were representative of the American housewife—forgetting for the moment that his wife runs a household where the annual income exceeds $10,000 and that the annual income of most American homes, even in "good times," is less than $3,000.

Let me tell you a true story of what happened in an important business conference not long ago.

A new package was being proposed for a product that had been on the market for years. The advertising-agency men were there, and the top executives of the company. All were waiting for the president of the company to open the meeting. All were anxious to hear what he thought of this new package. In due time the president pulled up his chair, cleared his throat once or twice, puffed on his cigar, observed the shining new package in the center of the table, and barked:

"Well, I think it's a lousy package."

There was a little nervous movement on the part of some of those around the table. A few of the company executives smiled, but the head of the art department of the advertising agency, who had designed the package, was plainly disturbed.

"Mr. Erwin," he ventured, meekly, "if I may I should like to point out that this new package is the result of a great deal of technical study. We have been very careful to see that the design has been well balanced." Then, reaching over, he picked up the package and went on to explain, "The illustration on this package, for example, is in harmony with the . . ."

"Well, I don't think it's so hot," the president cut in.

And that ended that.

Neither side even intimated that, after all, it didn't make any important difference what either of these men thought of the package—that its market success depended entirely on what the American housewife thought of it.

Salesmen often suffer financially from egocentric thinking. Their thoughts are likely to revolve so exclusively around themselves and their product that they are quite unequal to the task of seeing the problems of those whom they attempt to sell.

Remember the last automobile accident you were in?

Whose fault was it? Why, the other fellow's, of course. All of which proves that there are three sides to any question:

1. Your side
2. The other fellow's side
3. The truth.

It's interesting to watch how our views change with our personal interests. On one occasion, when a boy, I went fishing with three other boys. On the way to the river we decided that the "catch" should be pooled and divided equally among all of us. And I agreed wholeheartedly. I felt that it was absolutely fair and square. But during the course of the day, I found that I was leading the rest in the number of fish caught, and my attitude toward the whole proposition of dividing the catch began to change. By the time the day was over and there was no further chance of anyone else catching as many fish as I had, I became violently opposed to our original proposition, and told the boys that I couldn't understand why a good fisherman should be penalized because of the incompetence and bad luck of his associates.

Boys are like that. And when they grow up to be men their prejudices on economics and government are affected by the number of fish they catch. If they are unfortunate enough to catch little or no fish, their views are likely to be socialistic, but they can change from socialistic to capitalistic almost overnight, if they are fortunate enough to "catch a lot of fish."

Quite aside from our possessions, there are a number of prejudices that happen to infest our minds, simply because our thoughts revolve about the place in which we happen to have been born.

Two plus two equals four. All over the world you can get universal agreement on that. That's a truth anywhere.

The farther north you go the colder it gets. You can get general agreement on this as long as you stay north of the equator. (But even north of the equator, this statement isn't always true.)

The United States has fought a just cause in every war in which she has ever engaged, and all revolutionary movements by force are bad except the Revolution of the American Colonies against England. These statements would be accepted by most citizens of the United States. But the moment you cross the border into Mexico on the south or Canada on the north, you might expect to get some violent disagreement.

Special history books are written by each nation from its own point of view. The history of the War of 1812 taught in Canada is so different from the version taught in the United States, that you would scarcely believe them to be accounts of the same war.

Even within our own country the history of our Civil

War taught in Northern schools and that taught in Southern schools are not the same. I always thought that Robert E. Lee was a wild-eyed rebel until I had a chance to talk with a friend who learned his history below the Mason-Dixon line. No wonder Napoleon remarked that history is a set of lies agreed upon.

I lived in Austin, Texas, for two years. One bright June morning I rushed to the bank to get some money so that I could go out of town. But the bank was closed. "What! Has this bank folded?" I wondered. A Texan passing by advised me, "Why don't you know, sir? This is June third. Jeff Davis's birthday!" I almost said, "Well, who is Jeff Davis?"

And Lincoln's birthday passes unnoticed in the South.

California is the most wonderful state in the Union. You can go almost anywhere in the State of California and get substantial agreement with this statement.

San Francisco is still the greatest city on the west coast. With this statement I have found consistent agreement in the northern sections of California, but exhaustive studies that I have made [1] show that the moment you get south of Kingsburg, California, in the general direction of Los Angeles, or north of Ashland, Oregon, in the general direction of Portland, there appears a sudden change of attitude that is almost fanatical.

[1] See *The Law of Retail Gravitation*, by William J. Reilly.

When a boy, I noticed in a neighborhood club sponsored by the Republican party, one set of pictures of the "Greatest American Presidents" decorating the walls. But one day in a Democratic club near by I found an entirely different set of pictures. My parents were able to explain the one set, but I never got a satisfactory explanation of the other.

If you were born in a Christian home, you probably think that Sabbath is synonymous with Sunday. But you can get a difference of opinion on this subject merely by covering the East Side of New York. As a matter of fact, the Greek Sabbath falls on Monday, the Persian Sabbath on Tuesday, the Assyrian Sabbath on Wednesday, the Egyptian Sabbath on Thursday, the Turkish Sabbath on Friday, and the Jewish Sabbath, as most of us know, falls on Saturday.

When I was in the navy during World War I, I drifted into a library where I saw a huge globe. I looked at France, Italy, Germany, England, Russia. Then I gave it a twirl. And while the world revolved before me, this thought came:

ANYTHING THAT YOU BELIEVE *because* YOU WERE BORN IN A CERTAIN FAMILY, CITY, STATE, OR NATION, AND ARE IDENTIFIED WITH CERTAIN ECONOMIC, POLITICAL, EDUCATIONAL, SOCIAL, BUSINESS, OR RELIGIOUS INSTITUTIONS, IS A PREJUDICE AND OPEN TO QUESTION.

It isn't an easy truth to accept. But this thought will do more than anything I know of, to protect a person from the expensive prejudices of egocentric thinking.

These prejudices are the little things that build barriers between men, races, and nations.

These are the little things that cause us unhappiness in our personal as well as our business lives, that keep us from understanding the waves of emotion which make imaginary enemies out of other men and which, from time to time, destroy many of us in world conflicts.

These are the little things that cause us to acquire evidence that is one-sided and so to think one-sided instead of straight. These prejudices harden the arteries of our minds, and it is only by consciously trying to check them that we can protect ourselves against the creeping paralysis of environmental thinking.

OUR PHYSICAL CONDITION
AFFECTS OUR THINKING

Such common expressions as "Don't worry yourself sick" would indicate a fairly wide recognition of the fact that our thinking affects our physical condition. It is also well to recognize, however, that the reverse is true—our physical condition affects our thinking.

Our mental attitude varies not only with our general physical fitness, but more specifically with our condition at various times of the day. You know people who swing from optimistic heights to the depths of pessimism, depending on how they "feel." For others, the range is not so wide, but it is always there.

If we stop to review our thinking at various times of the day, we will probably discover that it is usually characterized by different mental attitudes at different times of the day. To a large extent this is due to variations in our physical condition.

Most of us are likely to pass confident judgments in the morning several hours after we have awakened, when we are fresh and relaxed. If we were called upon to pass judgments on the very same materials late in the afternoon, after a busy day, our judgments might be entirely different.

When we are relaxed, properly fed, at leisure, our thinking is likely to be at its best. On the other hand, when we are tense, tired, hungry, or in a hurry, we are likely to arrive at hasty judgments that are poor; we are likely to be irritable, unfair, and inconsiderate in our personal relations with others.

In many cases it is worth while for a person to review the type of thinking that he does at various times of the day, in an attempt to discover when he does his best mental work, and then to arrange his schedule so that he can handle the most important matters during these hours. Personally, I have found that I ordinarily do my best thinking in the middle of the morning and right after dinner in the evening, from about seven to eight. But I eat a light dinner.

WE LEARN BY EXPERIENCE MANY THINGS THAT ARE NOT SO

To "learn by experience" has been drummed into the minds of all of us, but we have not been sufficiently warned that we accumulate experience faster than we can digest it, and that without the proper study, experience will teach us a lot of things that are not so.

George Westinghouse was assured by the outstanding engineers of his day, all of whom had had a wealth of experience with brakes, that it was impossible to stop a train with air. They knew it by experience. Westinghouse himself, at that time, had not had that experience. "Reasons why it couldn't be done," therefore, did not discourage him, and we all know that he ultimately devised a successful air brake.

The man who sailed across the Atlantic in the *Santa Maria* was assured by those who "knew most about the earth" at that time, that the earth was flat and that he would at some point suddenly sail off the edge of a shelf into an utter abyss—into a swirling, boiling, bottomless pit filled with weird monsters. Then, for centuries after the time of Columbus, the master minds said that the world was round—that it was a sphere. Today we know that the world isn't a sphere.

21

Most of you probably know "by experience" that grass is green and that skies are blue. As a matter of fact, neither of these generalities is true.

Most of you know "by experience" that the more windows we have in a building, the better light we get. But when Simonds Saw Company built their plant and came to the problem of lighting, they stopped long enough to reason out that there is one best set of lighting conditions for any office or plant and that the real problem, therefore, is to secure *controlled* lighting that provides this set of conditions. Light from the outside varies from day to day and from hour to hour throughout any day. So that the only way to secure controlled lighting is by having no windows at all. That's the way the Simonds plant was built. That is the way a million-and-a-half-dollar Sears Roebuck windowless store in Chicago was built.

If anyone doubts that some pretty prominent architects have made the mistake of thinking that good lighting means lots of windows, let him check over some of the newer buildings here in New York.

It hasn't been many years ago that most of us knew "by experience" that the more windows we had in a building, the better air we would get. Now air-conditioning begins with sealing up all the windows.

If controlled air-conditioning and lighting can best be accomplished without any windows, then the only reasons I can see for having windows in a building at all are so that the employees can be disturbed and can look out when there is some noise in the street, or so that the executives can gaze out and daydream, or jump out if business gets too bad.

Business is full of antiquated policies for this or against that—policies that have been adopted as an outgrowth of early experiences.

It certainly is true that once we arrive at a decision as the result of experience, we cling to it tenaciously. We cling to it unless we are intellectually honest enough to admit that we made a mistake in arriving at that decision, or that our decision, even though correct when made, is no longer applicable, because conditions have changed.

I know several chief executives who prefer to employ men who have had no experience whatsoever in their kind of business.

OUR ATTITUDE TOWARD OTHER
PEOPLE AFFECTS OUR THINKING

There are many ways in which our attitude toward other people may affect our thinking.

It is interesting that when we are trying to make an impression on "equals" or "superiors," our judgments are likely to be studied and more than fair, but in dealing with persons whom we regard as "inferiors" we tend to be arbitrary or even dogmatic.

An idea originating with a chief executive may be accepted with little or no question, but the same idea, coming from a person working under you, is likely to receive less serious consideration—it may even be rejected in haste or entirely ignored.

We may think one way when we are complimented and another way when challenged or opposed. Whether we admit it or not, the fellow who compliments us at the start is much more likely to get us thinking with him.

We are much more likely to accept statements from people we like than from people we dislike, however reasonable or unreasonable those statements may be.

We are inclined to believe that what an older person says is wiser than what a younger person may say. We are awed by a gray beard. And yet I have never been able to discern any necessary relation between age and wisdom.

We are much more likely to accept the statements of an authority than we are to question them, even though that authority may be talking entirely outside the field in which he is recognized as being an authority. The opinions of Edison on education, and those of Ford on international relations, have gained wide but unwarranted acceptance largely because these men are known as authorities in other fields. It is certainly true that authorities, who make carefully reasoned and qualified statements when talking in their own field, are frequently guilty of generalizing and of making unsupported statements when talking outside their field.

There is one unique case which might well be studied by all of us because it provides such an excellent example of a man properly restricting himself to his own field, and that is the testimony of Colonel Lindbergh before the Senate during an air-mail probe.

Lindbergh merely advanced the simple and incontrovertible principle of justice that the air lines have a right to a hearing and a trial, saying, "I feel that it is so obvious that these companies were entitled to trial that it is not a legal question."

A careful study of his testimony reveals that he offered opinions only on questions bearing on the technical aspects of aviation and refused to comment on questions outside this, his chosen field. When asked how a proposed air-mail bill should be worded, he replied: "That isn't my field. I'm not familiar with legislation." When asked to suggest rates for carrying air mail, he said, "That is out of my field." When he had insufficient basis for an opinion on aviation policies of the previous administration, he refused to venture any, saying, "I am not sufficiently acquainted with details to give an opinion." When asked an "if" question in relation to subsidies involving an officer of his company, Lindbergh quickly identified it as an improper question, answering, "That's a hypothetical question and I don't feel I should answer it."

Most authorities, however, are not so careful about

25

restricting their opinions to matters within their own field. It is wise, therefore, to examine so-called "authoritative" statements before accepting them as a sound basis for your judgments.

SATISFYING OURSELVES THAT WE ARE RIGHT

It would be nice to believe that we think before we act. But we seldom do. Ordinarily we act first and then figure out good reasons why we behaved that way.

After we have made an important purchase, for example, it is so easy to invent or discover reasons why we made a wise choice.

The very day after I had bought a Buick I began to turn my neck at every Buick that passed on the highway. I began to "talk about" the Buick automobile with others who knew something about the mechanical features, etc. And from these conversations and observations that I made *after* I bought the car, I built up a convincing list of points which I found myself offering to everyone who asked me, as reasons why I had bought it in the first place.

In business, if a deal falls through, it is easy for us to figure out why "the other fellow is crazy." Whether profits turn up or down, it is a simple matter to arrive at an explanation that is very satisfactory to ourselves.

We compliment ourselves when everything goes along smoothly, and we think we are the victim of circumstances when things go wrong. When our business is good, we attribute it to good management; when our business is bad, we attribute it to the depression.

It's what the psychologist has been calling rationalization for a good many years now.

WE WOULD RATHER TELL THAN ASK

One of the most refreshing experiences in human life is to look into the eyes of a child who asks a question because he wants to learn. Most of us have forgotten how to ask a question. We like to appear "all-knowing." We don't enjoy admitting that we are ignorant about anything.

To illustrate, not long ago a man approached me in the subway station and made a flat statement, "This train goes to Wall Street,"—in much the same tone of voice as one uses when he says, "It is a nice day."

"Yes, it does," I answered, and went on looking at my paper.

But this fellow still hovered near by and finally opened up the conversation again. "It takes only about ten minutes to go down there," he asserted.

"No, it is more than that, probably nearer to twenty-five or thirty minutes," I answered. "You ought to change to the express at the second stop from here."

"The express doesn't stop here," he stated.

"No, this is a local station," I explained.

"I don't think it would be worth while to bother changing to the express."

"Well, you would save about ten or fifteen minutes," I told him.

"Wall Street is an express stop."

I nodded that it was, after which he said, "Well, thank you."

Here was a man obviously after information, but instead of asking questions, he simply made a series of statements, which apparently I was either to affirm or contradict. He made these statements with the air that he was simply confirming something he already knew about.

On one occasion I went with the president of a large sales organization to visit one of his district managers. Afterwards, the president said to me:

"I don't think that man will go much farther in our sales organization. He was so busy telling us how much he knew. Did you notice that he didn't ask us a single question?"

Merely to ask a question, however, does not necessarily mean that we have a desire to learn. Sometimes we ask questions just to make an impression or to be polite or because we want to have something to say.

A young lady once asked Dr. McCosh, one-time president of Princeton, a question on moral philosophy. He looked at her sharply, and said, "Madam, are you asking for information or just to make conversation?"

As we shall see later in our discussions, *intelligent* questioning occupies an important place in the rules for straight thinking.

WE STIFLE OUR NATIVE CURIOSITY

Because of our hesitancy to ask wide-open questions, whatever native curiosity we might have had becomes stifled. In fact, the typical lack of intellectual curiosity among adults has led some philosophers to conclude that most of us really have no sincere desire to learn. It is so easy to accept and take for granted the commonplace things that are around us.

One day as I passed the Morgan Private Library on Thirty-sixth Street in New York, the architectural beauty of the building with its cloistered appearance attracted me. Outside the heavy iron gates which guarded the entrance to the grounds stood an attendant.

"What's inside that building?" I asked.

He seemed surprised at first, then explained, "I've never been in there—I'm just the watchman."

"How long have you been watching this building?"

"Oh, for years," he replied, offhand. "But I've nothing to do with the inside—I don't know what's in there."

You are probably thinking, as I did, "Well, there's a dumb guy." But how many of us have been watching our business for years without ever generating sufficient curiosity to find out what really "makes the wheels go round"?

There are many cases in business in which manufacturers take their products for granted without being at all curious concerning how well or how poorly they satisfy the desires and wants of consumers for whom their product is supposed to be designed.

For example, a sheet manufacturer learned quite by accident from a housewife that his sheets—a well-known brand—were not long enough.

"The mister's feet come out at the bottom of the bed every night," she complained.

When this manufacturer took the trouble to get the measurements of a standard mattress, he was surprised to learn that his sheets really weren't long enough to be securely tucked under and still provide room enough for a person's feet.

A cooking-fat manufacturer, who was telling housewives in his advertisements how wonderful his product was for making biscuits, was told: "Don't tell me your product is wonderful for biscuits. You tell me to keep it in the ice-box. When I come downstairs in the morning, pull that stuff out of the ice-box and try to mix up some biscuits for breakfast, it is as hard as a rock. It won't mix." Not until this fact was brought to the attention of the manufacturer did he make his product easier to mix at ice-box temperature.

In a recent conference I listened to a heated argument

over what magazines should be used to advertise a certain product. After both sides had got tired and the meeting was about to break up, I asked the same old question: "Who uses your product and where do they live? Maybe that would have something to do with what magazines are to be used—if they are to be used at all."

No one at the meeting knew specifically; one said his wife used it, another mentioned a friend. A third said that the "better" classes used it, and then an entirely new argument boiled between him and the sales manager, who contended that "everybody" used it.

It's incredible that manufacturers know so little about their markets, but few seem to have sufficient curiosity to go out and find out what these markets consist of— specifically, who uses their product and what they think of it. Consequently, they have no adequate conception of what their real marketing problems are or what their sales objectives ought to be.

Common Mistakes in Thinking

There are certain typical and well-defined mistakes commonly found in our everyday thinking. The best protection against these common mistakes is to become so well acquainted with them that we are able quickly to detect and to identify them in our own thinking, as well as in the thinking of others.

MISTAKING THE UNIQUE FOR THE TYPICAL

Mistaking the unique for the typical is an easy error to fall into. One company, for example, received hundreds of letters from consumers explaining how good their product was for cleaning false teeth. The company got all excited about it, and immediately wanted to spend some money featuring the product in an entirely new package for this purpose. As a matter of fact, the use of the product for false teeth was unique. That's the reason consumers wrote to the company about it. And a few hundred letters, after all, were not very many when one considered that millions of consumers were using the product for regular everyday, typical, large-volume purposes which were so commonplace that consumers would never think of writing in to the company telling about such accepted uses.

On one occasion I sent out a mail questionnaire and then went out personally and interviewed those who answered the questionnaire and those who did not answer, in an attempt to find out whether or not there were any significant differences between the two groups. In this case it was found that 92 per cent of those who answered the questionnaire were users of the product involved. But only 40 per cent of those who had not answered were users of the product.

In other words, to have taken the results of those

who answered as typical of the whole would have been very misleading.

"Anecdotal reasoning"—telling a story to drive home a point—is so often subject to the mistake of representing a unique happening as a typical one. This type of reasoning is extensively and effectively used by those who sell—even by those who know better—because they know that it is one of the favorite indoor sports of those who buy, many of whom don't like "statistics," but prefer to hear what Grocer Schultz in Cincinnati thinks, or what happened to Mrs. DePan at the bridge tea.

If you watch the thinking of others, and perhaps your own, you will observe how often some anecdote is used to "prove" a case. Such anecdotes are frequently based on experiences which have left a lasting impression on our minds because they were *unique*. Typical happenings are more likely to go unnoticed.

DRAWING GENERAL CONCLUSIONS
FROM LIMITED EVIDENCE

As soon as we acquire a few bits of evidence on almost any subject, we are naturally inclined to feel obliged to arrive at some conclusion. We get into bad habits of expressing general opinions just to "make conversation."

When a person returns from a summer in Europe, for example, and is questioned by his friends about his experiences abroad, his natural inclination is to expand himself and to talk in an "authoritative" manner about "conditions" in Europe.

Recently I talked with a young man who had fallen in love. He has written a poem about "love" and is now writing a novel about "women." I suggested that what he really ought to write about is his love-affair with Sadie Martin in Lima, Ohio, under certain weather conditions, with her folks out of town, etc., and that it is a mistake in thinking for him to assume that his love-affair with Miss Martin gives him sufficient grounds on which to generalize about "love" or about "women."

Early one September I had a four-page closely type-written communication from a young applicant for a job who wrote that he had graduated from college in June and then had spent July and August touring the country in order to get a thorough grasp of the "economic situation" before applying for a job.

One of our leading business associations was holding its annual convention. A report on an old controversial issue of national importance was brought up for comment. Immediately the floor was the scene of vehement discussion. After most of the gentlemen had got the gas off their stomachs, the chairman asked for a show of hands on who had actually read the report. Only about 10 per cent had read it.

At luncheon a friend recently told me that he had just returned from a trip throughout the Middle West and he proceeded to explain the "attitude of business leaders" in that section of the country. Toward the end of the conversation, I found that my friend's trip throughout the "Middle West" consisted of three days at Chicago, one day in Cincinnati, and one day in Pittsburgh, and involved personal contacts with about a dozen men who were primarily interested in the tobacco business.

To anyone on the lookout for this mistake in thinking, it soon becomes apparent that our everyday conversations provide an abundance of examples that show how easy and how common it is for a person to jump to general conclusions on the basis of evidence which is fragmentary and incomplete.

Some one has said that the narrower the mind, the broader the statement.

ASSUMING SIMILAR OBJECTS OR SITUATIONS ARE ALIKE IN ALL RESPECTS

How common it is for us to make the mistake of assuming that objects or situations that are alike in some respects are alike in all respects.

It is easy to think of a number of simple examples. In surveying markets, we are inclined to bracket together cities of around the same population as if they were alike in relation to all important factors that affect the sale of the product involved. In studying advertising media we compare circulation figures for different publications, even though we know that they are not comparable in light of significant differences in the nature of coverage and readership for the individual product we have in mind.

Or take a case in sales analysis. Suppose, in reviewing sales trends in different territories, we were to find out, as one company did, that per capita sales had declined about the same amount, within the past two years, in seven out of sixty-two territories. We would be likely to group these seven territories together, as this company did, and assume that they all represented about the same kind of situation and required about the same kind of treatment. Upon examination, however, the danger of treating these seven territories, with the same per capita decline, as if they were alike in all respects, becomes quite obvious when we realize that a given decrease in per capita consumption may be the result of one or more of the five following conditions:

(1) Possibly *fewer* customers are using the product at about the *same rate* as those who had been using it before.

(2) Possibly *fewer* customers are using *less* of the product.

(3) Possibly *fewer* customers are using *more* of the product per customer, but there is sufficient decline in the number of them using the product to decrease the per capita consumption of the territory as a whole.

(4) Possibly the *same number* of customers are using the product, but are using *less* of the product than before.

(5) Possibly *more* customers are using the product, but are using a sufficiently small *amount* of the product to decrease the amount used per capita for the territory as a whole.

36

Our habit of assuming that objects or situations that are alike in some respects are alike in all respects is due to the fact that we have not trained our mind's eye consciously and deliberately to look for differences as well as for similarities.

If you want a little practice along this line, take any two related objects, such as a pen and a pencil, and list the respects in which they are the same from the standpoint of dimensions, materials, uses. Then list the respects in which they are different. Some people have what is called a "dissimilarity" mind; in other words, they are likely to notice the respects in which two objects or situations are *unlike*. On the other hand, other people have a "similarity" mind and are more likely to notice the respects in which objects or situations are *alike*. Before your point of view can be called either balanced or intelligent, however, you must be able to see both similarities and dissimilarities. And a little practice along the line indicated will bring such a point of view about.

OVERLOOKING DIFFERENCES IN TIME

We are continually losing sight of the dimension of time. We assume that a condition which existed at a certain time was at some previous time, is now, or will be at some later time, necessarily the same.

Last winter when I was in southern California several

friends who had not been East for a number of years pointed out how much more modern women's bathing suits are in California. They involved themselves in the mistaken assumption that women were wearing the same kind of bathing suits in the East as they used to.

Four years ago a manufacturer made a study of his product uses and gathered some extremely valuable data, but now makes the mistake of continuing to use that information, even though several new uses for the product have come into the picture and *may* account for a large share of the total present-day consumption.

Recently I was present when a sales manager called a salesman on the carpet and bawled him out for not reaching his quota, saying: "The trouble must be with you, Donnelly. I traveled that territory for eleven years and I know what's in it." But it had been *seven* years since the sales manager last traveled the territory. Nevertheless, the salesman's quota was based on conditions in the territory "as the sales manager knew them." As a matter of fact, the potential market had shrunk in that territory while it had gained in others.

After all, "the world do move, it do." We are continually saying it. But we are continually forgetting it. In spite of all the talk of our living in a dynamic world, we are inclined to think as if conditions stayed put.

38

ASSUMING OPPOSITES

When one is unable to prove a proposition, we are likely to accept this inability as proof that the opposite is true. In law, a prosecuting attorney's inability to prove the defendant guilty of murder, and the defendant's consequent acquittal, leads us to feel that the defendant has been "vindicated" and his innocence "proved."

Every time any nation has ever gone off the gold standard, there have been those who have contended that unsatisfactory economic conditions which followed were largely due to the change, apparently forgetting that conditions were unsatisfactory before the change was made. Just because proponents of the new program are unable to *prove* that the change is a wise one, opponents are likely to take this inability as being proof that the old order was better. On the other hand, friends of the new program throw the burden of proof on their critics, saying "conditions are better than they would have been," and the inability of their critics to prove otherwise is taken by proponents as proof that the new order is better.

Similarly, every time anyone in business suggests a new method of distribution, or a new advertising plan, or a change in administrative practice, in fact, any kind of change, he is likely to meet the opposition of those who ask him to prove his case in advance. And his inability to do so is usually taken by his opponents as being conclusive evidence that it would be unwise to make the change. On the other hand, he and his supporters believe that his plan would work because opponents can't prove that it wouldn't.

Instead of throwing the burden of proof back and forth on a question that cannot be proved one way or the other in advance, how much more intelligent it would be for both sides to say, "We don't know how the plan would work until we try it," and then decide, as a practical matter, whether or not the plan deserves a trial. But they seldom do.

The next time anyone suggests a new course of action in our business, political, social, or religious life, look out for this common mistake in the thinking on both sides.

MISAPPLYING GENERAL RULES

Applying a general rule to a case which appears to belong, but which actually does not belong, under that rule, is another mistake in thinking often encountered.

The owner of a department store wrongly assumed that it was all right for his business to be 18 per cent behind last year's simply because a general business index was off 18 per cent.

A grocery manufacturer arrived at a general rule that it would be better to sell direct rather than through jobbers. But when he proceeded to apply this general rule to sparse territories such as the Minneapolis-St. Paul territory and Texas, it turned out that these markets presented conditions which did not belong under the general rule, and that it would be far better to sell through jobbers there. The company had overlooked significant differences in these territories, and consequently misapplied the general rule to them.

We may start out with the general rule that cutting expenses is the best way to increase profits. And yet there may be a number of items under the head of production, or sales, or advertising, which, if cut, would decrease profits.

The credit manager of a large department store found that three other stores in town were securing profitable increases by introducing more liberal credit requirements. It looked like a general rule that "easing up on credit requirements would secure profitable increases." But he overlooked the fact that his store was dealing with a different class of people, and before he woke up he had lost some money. He, like the others mentioned, had made the mistake of applying a general rule to a case which appeared to belong, but which actually did not belong, under that rule.

ASSUMING EXCLUSIVE CAUSAL RELATIONS

Our great desire to "explain things" leads us to assume that one condition is responsible for another, when there are many other factors involved.

General business conversations are full of examples of this mistake. Nearly everyone has his own favorite reason and explanation for present "business conditions." Seldom do we hear a balanced statement that makes any attempt at recognizing the many and varied contributing factors.

No matter what happens in your own business, you can usually depend upon each person involved developing his own explanation, which unduly emphasizes one or two or three factors in the situation to the practical exclusion of many other points which should be considered.

Sometimes our desire to "claim credit" or to "avoid blame" leads us to assume exclusive causal relations. Salesmen and buyers alike fall victim on this score. For example, an advertising campaign in a national magazine was followed by gains in the advertiser's sales and profits. The salesman for that medium proceeded to talk about the campaign as if it were primarily responsible for the company's gains—largely overlooking the effects of additional sales work and of other contributory marketing efforts.

In another instance, an extensive national advertising campaign was not followed by expected gains. The advertiser blamed the publications used and the advertising agency—overlooking at the time the fact that there are a number of elements involved in the sale of any product. There are, in addition to advertising, the product itself, the price of the product, the availability of the product, personal selling, and a wide variety of factors affecting the market for the product, all of which have something to do with sales increases or decreases. And in addition to all this, the activities of competitors, as they apply these same marketing instruments, have some effect on all a company does.

DRAWING FAULTY COMPARISONS

The last common mistake in thinking that will be mentioned here is that of drawing comparisons based on conditions that are not the same.

Everyone knows the old joke, that "black horses eat more than white horses," a puzzling condition which is finally cleared up by the statement that "there are more black horses." The unequal basis of comparison is so obvious in this case that it makes a good joke. But very few of us realize how commonly we become involved in mistakes in thinking that are based on the same fundamental point.

A business man may observe figures that show that

the sales of a grocery chain have increased this month in comparison with the same month last year, without stopping to question whether the sales are based on the same number of stores.

Or a direct-mail advertiser, noting an increase in the *cost* of inquiries from a given magazine, may conclude that the magazine is losing its pulling power, without realizing that he is comparing his costs on the basis of conditions which are not comparable. He may be slowly exhausting the prospects reached by that circulation, or, because of an increase in competitive advertising, he may be getting a smaller share of those prospects. Or general conditions in the market may be such that this type of advertising generally is pulling less in nearly all publications.

It might be interesting, in reviewing the last few paragraphs, to note that every one of the cases offered probably seemed so obvious to you when it was mentioned that you thought to yourself, "Well, I'd never make a mistake like that!"

But if you will take the time to examine all of the "more now than there used to be" or "less now than there used to be" statements, that you make within the next few days, I believe you will be surprised to learn how frequently you become involved in mistaken comparisons that are based on conditions which are not the same.

One of the main reasons why all of us are guilty of the common mistakes in thinking that have just been discussed, is that we think we do not make them. If we take the time to become familiar with them, however, we will not only recognize how frequently we all make them, but we will be in a favorable position to detect, and to a large extent eliminate, these mistakes.

But, after all, an examination of these faulty mental attitudes and common mistakes in thinking merely shows us what *not* to do. They are the *negative* things we must avoid.

So let's be off on our exploration of the *positive* steps that must be made. Let us proceed with the examination of our second main question, "What are the positive rules for straight thinking and how can I learn to use them?"

CHAPTER THREE

Reducing Straight Thinking
to Four Simple Steps

IN ATTEMPTING TO REDUCE THE JOB OF STRAIGHT THINK-
ing to a few simple chronological steps, our best cue
comes from the scientific laboratory. Most of us are
probably familiar with the traditional four-step reasoning usually employed by those who labor there.

*Step 1. Some kind of observation suggests an unan-
swered question or a problem.*

For example, the superintendent of a paper plant goes
to the chief of the testing laboratory, saying, "Look at
the little flaws in this paper. Every once in a while we
get a run like this—and the paper is more brittle than
it should be."

*Step 2. The problem is defined and possible solutions
considered.*

In an attempt to define his problem and to visualize
the various factors that might be responsible for this
faulty and brittle paper, the scientist begins to ask a
series of questions, such as:

46

"When did this faulty paper begin to appear?"

"Are all machines involved or just part of them?"

"When did it occur before?"

"Where have we been getting our raw materials during these periods?"

"Who was running the paper-machines when these faults occurred?"

"Has the speed at which the machines are run anything to do with these faults?"

Until finally he feels able to mold these questions into a well-rounded and comprehensive definition of his problem, with all possible causes taken into account. Such a statement might be, "What factors related to raw materials, machinery, labor, or atmospheric conditions in the plant are responsible for this faulty and brittle paper?"

The scientist then lists the various conditions that might be responsible for the faulty paper, and selects one or more that seem most likely, and inquires into them first.

Step 3. Controlled experiments are set up and observations made.

If, in the example given, the scientist suspects raw materials as the most likely cause, he conducts a laboratory analysis of these materials in search for the troublesome elements. If the results of this analysis give no satisfactory or complete answer, and the scientist suspects the operation of the machines, he may conduct experimental runs at different speeds and under different conditions. And so the systematic collection of evidence continues until the basic causes are tracked down.

Step 4. A conclusion is drawn based on the results of experimental and other observations.

These four scientific steps in straight thinking, together with the path of the one-track mind, are shown in a simple chart on the following page.

From this chart we see that the first step in straight thinking has to do with *expansion*—the expansion of an original idea, or impression, or observation as it enters the mind, so that we get a full factual view of it from the standpoint of *what, when, where,* and *who.*

Next, the chart presents the second step in straight thinking as one of *contraction*—the contraction of your full observation into a precise and analytical definition of your real problem. This definition provides the basis for your consideration of possible solutions and leads to Step 3.

Step 3 again has to do with *expansion*—the expansion of your mental horizons to include all available positive and negative evidence in relation to each possible solution.

Step 4, the final step, has to do with *contraction*, inasmuch as it leads to the elimination of the least

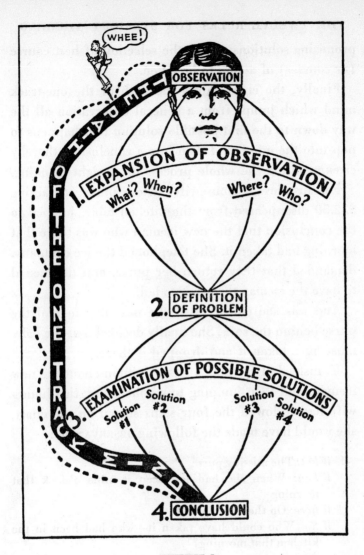

EXHIBIT I

promising solutions and to the selection of best course (or courses) of action to be taken.

Finally, the chart shows the path of the one-track mind which jumps from a general observation all the way down to the first possible solution that happens to pop into the mind, and then into a conclusion, thereby circumventing the whole process of straight thinking.

For instance, a housewife, whose purse containing $32.50 disappeared from the kitchen table, jumped to the conclusion that the new iceman who was there that morning had taken it. She telephoned the ice company, demanded that they return her purse, and threatened to have the iceman thrown into jail.

And was she embarrassed the next day to find the purse behind the sofa! She finally decided that the baby must have taken it and dropped it there.

If, instead of forming a hasty opinion about the new iceman, and then jumping to a conclusion, this housewife had followed the four steps shown on the chart, she would have made the following OBSERVATION:

I. *What:* The missing purse

   When: When she had last seen it, nine o'clock that morning

   Where: On the kitchen table

   Who: Who could have taken it—who had been in the kitchen that morning?

II. She would have DEFINED HER PROBLEM:

   "To try to determine how the purse had come to disappear."

III. She would have taken an open-minded approach, giving
due CONSIDERATION TO such POSSIBLE SOLUTIONS as:

    1. She herself may have absent-mindedly mislaid it

    2. The baby might have carried it away

    3. The iceman might have taken it and the search she
       naturally would make in examining solutions 1 and
       2 would have led to her finding the purse and to

IV. the CONCLUSION that the baby had dropped it behind the
sofa. And so she would have saved herself the embarrassment of having unjustly accused the iceman.

Here's another one:

A husband, reviewing the family financial situation,
jumped to the conclusion that his wife was getting extravagant and careless with his money and he didn't
waste any time telling her so. "We used to get along
nicely on three hundred dollars a month," he barked.
"Now we hardly seem able to get by on four hundred
dollars!"

After the smoke of battle had cleared away and both
of them had said a lot of nasty things they didn't mean,
which left his wife in a sobbing spell, he found himself
defeated and considerably embarrassed. He had tem-
porarily overlooked certain obvious facts—that two
children had been born in the family since "they used
to get along on $300," that the three other children
had grown up some and that the price level had
risen.

He could easily have avoided the nasty quarrel and

his subsequent embarrassment if, instead of taking one long jump on an opinion, he had

1. OBSERVED *what* the money was being spent for, *when* it was being spent, *where* it was being spent, and for *whom.* In the process of answering these questions, the facts that he had overlooked on the growth of the family would have come to the surface. Then, with these facts at hand, it would have been a simple matter for him to sit down with his wife and to
2. DEFINE THEIR PROBLEM of trying to cut expenses,
3. EXAMINE THE VARIOUS POSSIBLE SOLUTIONS for doing so, and to
4. ARRIVE AT A CONCLUSION on the best ways and means of cutting expenses.

Sometimes a person loses his life by jumping to a conclusion. A West Virginia woman died an hour after she had jumped through a window, thinking that her home was burning, when actually the house next door had caught fire.

These simple cases may leave you with the feeling that you would never make mistakes like these. And maybe not. But after all, highly intelligent people sometimes jump to conclusions on the basis of inadequate evidence.

It even happened to the Chief Justice of the Supreme Court of the United States. On election night, 1916, Charles Evans Hughes retired believing himself the next President of the United States. A little after midnight a newspaperman called to tell him that California was in doubt.

"The President cannot be disturbed," announced young Charles Hughes, Jr.

The newspaperman persisted.

"You will have to come back in the morning; the President cannot be disturbed."

"Well, when he wakes up just tell him that he isn't President," the reporter replied.[1]

In order to simplify as much as possible the actual performance of the four steps in straight thinking, and in order to express them in such a way that they can be readily understood and easily applied, we can break them down into twelve elementary rules which, if followed, will straighten out anyone's thinking on any problem he may encounter. In other words, there are only twelve simple rules under four main steps to be followed if you want to think straight on any subject.

These rules will teach you how to form intelligent opinions and to make sound decisions.

When we are merely daydreaming, it is unnecessary to have any plan or direction to our thoughts. But when we are attempting to arrive at a decision concerning some plan of action to be followed, our thoughts had better follow a certain prescribed course. And the purpose of the rules for straight thinking is to guide one along that course. Trained minds do not blunder into achievement; they plan it.

[1] From *The Nine Old Men,* by Drew Pearson and Robert S. Allen.

The rules will help you to express your opinions, feelings, beliefs, and decisions in a clear, logical, and straightforward fashion that cannot help but earn the respect of your social and business associates.

But the rules will do more than straighten out your own thinking. Once mastered, they will help you quickly to detect flaws in the opinions and arguments of others, and to call the attention of others to these flaws in an intelligent way.

Without a knowledge of the rules, you may listen to the arguments of someone else, feel intuitively that "there is something wrong" in the other person's reasoning, but, because you are unable to identify the fault specifically, you begin shooting blindly in the air with general objections and get hopelessly tangled in an endless argument. On the other hand, a thorough acquaintance with the rules permits you to put your finger on the mistake. Then and not until then are you in an intelligent position to devise some simple inoffensive and diplomatic way of giving the conversation an entirely new start that avoids the fault and reopens the other person's mind.

Merely to read the rules, however, is not to master them, any more than to read the rules on swinging a golf club or playing bridge is to master either of these games. Mastery comes through continuous practice. The inclination, even after you are fairly well acquainted with the rules, will be to fall into old habits of thinking. But if you use the rules in your thinking day in and day out, you will, in a remarkably short time, build them into your mental habits, with the result that your mental processes will become straight automatically.

Before the rules for playing bridge were simplified and made generally available, it was quite difficult for the average person to play a very good game. But now that most of the plays have been identified so that general rules may be safely followed, there are millions of people who play a pretty good hand of bridge.

Similarly, the fundamentals of golf have been simplified to such a degree that by following the rules the average person can, with a reasonable amount of practice, shoot a fair game.

But it is far more difficult to teach the rules to a man who has been playing golf for years in his own way, than it is to teach a beginner who has never had a golf club in his hand. The first man has so much to unlearn.

As far as our mental operations are concerned, all of us have been engaged in some brand or other of thinking as far back as we can remember. We have acquired many habitual modes of thinking that are illogical. Over a period of years, the doors of our minds and the chambers within have become overrun and tangled with the underbrush of prejudices, beliefs, convictions, and opinions, which bar our easy reception of the truth and choke our ability to think straight.

As long as our mind is not hermetically sealed, however, it can be slowly and completely opened, preconceptions can be cleared away, expensive grooves of habit can be regularly massaged until they have practically disappeared.

Now that we have had a preview of what to do and what not to do in our thinking, we shall unfold the four steps in orderly thinking more slowly, devoting one complete chapter to the rules under each step, so that we may fully understand the elementary steps of an orderly mind.

CHAPTER FOUR

Making Precise Observations

STRAIGHT THINKING starts with facts. Careless thinking starts with opinions. And every day of our lives we mix them up without realizing it.

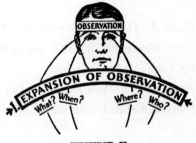

EXHIBIT II

If we were to begin today to form the habit of making a mental note of those statements which we hear in the course of our conversations with friends and associates, we would probably be utterly amazed at the high percentage of such statements which are without adequate foundation. Many of these statements are merely opinions. Even when facts are included in a statement, they are so often loosely combined with opinions or impressions—clearly demonstrating that the person responsible for the statement has made no conscious effort to *discriminate* between the two.

Such discrimination is the central thought behind the first rule under the head of "Making Precise Observations."

Precise observation, however, goes one step further than mere discrimination. It also involves analysis, as stated in Rule 2.

Rules for Making Precise Observations

Rule 1. Define the primary facts in connection with your observation, and separate these facts from any opinions or impressions.

Rule 2. Analyze the facts, as far as they will permit, from the standpoint of what, when, where, and who.

If, in analyzing our facts, we overlook any one of the four W's, What, When, Where, and Who, we may wind up with inaccurate and confusing results. My conversation with a Polish woman taught me that.

Back in 1920, helping the Census Bureau to count how many people there were in the United States, I had a misunderstanding in a Polish neighborhood in Pittsburgh.

At one door I asked a mother how many children she had.

"A-fife!" she replied.

"Give me their names, please, in the order of their age, the eldest first," I requested.

"Stashu, Manyu, Stefania, Ignace, Elitsia, and Stanislaus."

"How many children did you say you had?" I asked, a little confused.

"A-fife!"

"Four boys and two girls, is that right?" I asked.

"A-shure!"

"But that makes six!" I exclaimed.

"Oh—axcuse plees! Two's a twin!"

The only difference between this Polish lady's observation and mine was that hers was a general observation and mine was an analytical one.

Thinking of "when," she had overlooked "who."

Motorists frequently overlook one or more of the four W's.

A lady from New Jersey was recalling a motor trip through the Middle West.

"Aren't the roads terrible in Ohio?" she commented.

"Why, I think the Ohio roads are grand!" replied a woman from Texas, who had also driven through the Buckeye State.

Both of them were dealing with facts. Both had driven across Ohio. But one of them had driven from Cincinnati to Cleveland three years ago, and the other had recently skirted the southern end of the state.

In addition to all this, the lady from New Jersey was comparing Ohio roads with the section of New Jersey in which she lived, which happens to have some of the newest and most modern roads in the country, whereas the lady from Texas was comparing the Ohio roads with those in the part of West Texas where she hailed from.

If they had stopped to consider for a moment *who* they were, they would have realized that because they came from different parts of the country where road conditions were widely different, they had altogether different standards for defining *what* a good road is. Because they drove over different roads in Ohio, they weren't talking about the same *where*. Because they had driven there at different times, they weren't talking about the same *when*.

Now let's take a business example.

What the President Said

A large food manufacturer sells his product in two forms through the usual grocery jobber and chain outlets. I asked the president, "Where are your sales strongest and where are they weakest?"

I wanted to know where sales were at their best and at their worst. For where sales are best, one is likely to discover those factors which are helping the business, and where sales are lowest, those conditions which are retarding the business.

This is what he said,

"I've been reviewing our sales figures for various census zones, and find that our sales are increasing and are strongest in the Mid-Atlantic States,[1] but are declining and are way off in the East North Central States.[2]

"Our per capita sales never have been so good in the Middle West as in the East, but instead of getting better out there they are getting worse. Of course, the purchasing power has held up better in the East, I think. The main trouble, though, with our Mid-Western States is that some of our sharp-shooting competitors are cutting prices all to pieces. I stopped in three or four stores in Fort Wayne and they are almost giving the stuff away. If we could only bring those Mid-Western States up to our Eastern level, we'd be sitting pretty. But one thing's sure, we've got to do something about it. We've got to put on more pressure out there in those five states."

Applying the first rule to this problem—defining the facts and separating them from opinions—we find that the primary facts are:

1. That total sales for the East North Central States have declined.
2. That total sales for the Mid-Atlantic States have increased.
3. That the president has said that he will have to "do something about it."

The rest of the material is merely assumption, opinion, or impression, as follows:

[1] Which include New York, New Jersey, and Pennsylvania.
[2] Which include Ohio, Indiana, Illinois, Michigan, and Wisconsin.

1. To say that the decline in sales in the Mid-West is largely due to price-cutting is, of course, an unsupported opinion. In the first place, the few cases of price-cutting observed in Fort Wayne are indefinite and do not support a conclusion that price-cutting is general throughout the East North Central States. In the second place, even though price-cutting were general throughout these states, it would be a mistake to assume any exclusive causal relation between this competitive price-cutting and a sudden decline in the sale of the company's product.

2. To say that sales have remained at a relatively high level in the East because the purchasing power of the East has held up better than in the West, is another unsupported opinion. In the first place, there is insufficient evidence to support the president's impression that purchasing power in the East has held up better than in the West. In the second place, even though it had, it would be a mistake to assume any exclusive causal relation between the general condition of purchasing power and sustained sales on this particular company's product.

3. The statement that more pressure is necessary in the Mid-West is based on the assumption that because the total sales for all five states have shown a decline, sales are off in every one of those five states.

4. To say that more pressure would result in increased sales and would correct the condition responsible for the decline in sales, is an assumption.

Now we are ready for the application of Rule 2—the analysis of the facts from the standpoint of what, when, where, and who—as it was followed in an actual analysis of this situation.

First, we analyzed the increasing sales in the Mid-Atlantic States.

What—This manufacturer is selling his product in two forms, A and B. So that instead of selling one product, he is really selling two products and they should be analyzed as such. A separation of these figures showed that sales on one form, A, had decreased, while sales on the other form, B, had increased sufficiently to cause the total sales figure to increase.

When—The analysis from the standpoint of When showed that these two sales trends extended back over a period of the past ten years.

Where—An analysis by states of increasing sales on Form B showed that they were not increasing in Pennsylvania and New Jersey, but only in New York State. Then separating New York State into (1) New York City and (2) the remainder of the state, it was found that sales were not increasing in the latter, but only in the New York City territory.

Who—An analysis of sales by types of jobbers in New York City territory showed that sales were not increasing among all types, but primarily among those who served the Jewish outlets.

Then, personal interviews among Jewish consumers revealed that the product was particularly acceptable to them because it had no animal fat in it and was therefore "kosher."

So that what was called an increase in sales in the Mid-Atlantic States turned out to be a marked increase in sales on one form of the product to one class of jobber and one class of consumer in one territory.

Similar analysis of the declining sales in the East North Central States revealed that a sudden drop in sales occurred about six months previous to our analysis, that both forms of the product were involved in the drop, that the drop was confined to one large chain-store organization in the city of Chicago. Finally, a telephone inquiry revealed that during the month our sales figures for Chicago showed a drop, this chain organization had changed its warehousing system whereby it discontinued distributing from a central warehouse in Chicago and began to distribute through local warehouses, many of which were outside of the East North Central States area.

So that what appeared to be a decline in sales in the East North Central States turned out to be a relocation of shipments by one large chain organization in one territory. This case never got past the first step in straight thinking.

One of the main purposes of the rules for precise observation is to protect us from the danger of starting out in our thinking with a false premise. For if the initial observation is wrong, everything that follows will necessarily be wrong. If we accept a false observation as a starting-point, the definition of our problem—which is the second step in orderly thinking—will be altogether wrong.

How Salesmen Go Wrong

In selling, the salesman so often gets a mistaken idea of what his sales problem really is, if he observes incorrectly—*i.e.*, if he accepts without question what a prospect tells him.

Years ago, when I was selling pressure cookers from door to door, I learned not to believe a housewife when she told me she hadn't any money.

Not long ago an insurance salesman told me that he lost a $100,000 policy because he believed a prospect who told him that he was getting a divorce from his wife and arranging to marry again, and that he was under too heavy an expense to consider insurance at that time. A few weeks later this salesman learned that the prospect had bought a $100,000 policy from another agent who apparently forgot about the "no money" objection and inspired the prospect to buy.

A publication representative, new on the job, called on a national advertiser who had used the publication some years before, and was advised by the advertising manager that the last campaign in this publication had failed and that consequently he would not be interested in trying it again.

One would naturally assume that an executive as well informed as the advertising manager knows what he is talking about. For five years other salesmen, calling on this same account, had accepted the advertising manager's contention without question, with the result that they looked upon that problem as being one of *attempting to resell a publication that had failed.* The new salesman, however, rather than accept this observation of the advertising manager, proceeded to follow the two rules for precise observation, dug into the advertiser's old sales records, asked the what, when, where, and who questions, with the result that he discovered certain statistical errors in the advertiser's summary of that campaign, presented the whole case to the advertiser, who saw that he had done the publication an injustice. Once this was brought to light, the sales problem was merely one of answering a few minor objections on the type of people reached by the publication, and when this was done, the advertiser resumed his use of the publication.

A machinery salesman called on the purchasing agent and was told:

"We don't want any more of your machines in our mill. The last one we bought from you broke down. We have a research department that carefully checks the relative performance of various makes of machines, and we have been instructed by our Director of Research not to buy any more of yours."

One would think that when the Director of Research of a large company, noted for its scientific work, reports that he has carefully checked the performance of a given machine and found it to be inferior to other competing machines, he knows what he is talking about.

But the machinery salesman, rather than accept even the word of a Director of Research, determined to look into the case. He proceeded to ask the what, when, where, and who questions. He talked with every employee who had had anything to do with operating the machine, and finally, in his conversation with the man on the night shift, learned that this operator had overloaded the machine in an emergency. When this evidence was brought to the attention of the purchasing agent, and through him to the Director of Research, the ban was lifted and about a month later, when they were ordering new machines, this salesman got his share of the business.

This case shows that even the Director of Research of a large scientific institution isn't always right.

These cases should be sufficient to demonstrate that when a salesman accepts without question what a prospect says, he builds up imaginary fears and hurdles in his mind which actually do not exist. They show that when he accepts the prospect's word—even the word of a Director of Research—he may start out with the wrong conception of what his selling problem really is. And how can anyone solve a sales problem, or any other kind of problem, unless he knows what it is?

In all our relations with other people, we are attempting to sell ideas of one kind or another. And it is impossible for us to have an accurate understanding of any problem unless we have made accurate observations to begin with. To start with an inaccurate observation will result either in a misconception of our problem or in the futile pursuit of a solution to a problem which doesn't even exist.

Case of John A. Manufacturer

Now let's take an example of a sound business observation that represents a real problem, and carry it through all the four steps in straight thinking.

John A. Manufacturer observed from his records that sales were steadily declining in the Chicago territory. In this case, there was no mistake about the observation. A hasty inquiry from the standpoint of what, when, where, and who, revealed that his soap chips were being displaced by a local competitor, that this displacement had been going on ever since the competing product was introduced about a year before, that John A.'s losses had extended to all sections of the Chicago territory where this competing product was sold, and that housewives gave as their reasons for changing brands that the competing brand "gives more suds," "works faster," and "goes farther."

Here, then, is an observation that is both accurate and specific and that gives rise to a real problem.

At the end of the next chapter we shall see how John A. defined his problem and considered possible solutions.

CHAPTER FIVE

Defining the Real Problem and
Considering Possible Solutions

WE HAVE NOW SEEN
that when we turn the
light of analysis on
our early observations,
many of our "prob-
lems" prove themselves
to be imaginary and
non-existent. Real prob-
lems, on the other hand,
show themselves in
clear relief under such
treatment, so that we

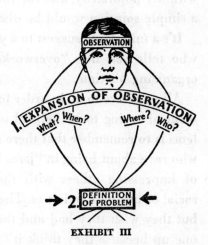

EXHIBIT III

can construct a precise and analytical definition of each
problem from the standpoint of what, when, where, and
who.

At the outset, however, let's be aware that many of
the so-called problems which arise in the usual course
of everyday conversation, are not to be looked upon as
problems at all, and it sometimes proves highly embar-
rassing for us to treat them as if they were.

When some sweet young thing says: "I don't know *what* to do. I've had this date with George for tonight and Tom is in from New Haven. I just *can't* make any excuses to Tom, and yet I wouldn't offend George for the world. What would you do?"

This young lady doesn't really want your help on a problem. What she's really trying to do is impress you with her popularity, and for you to come right out with a simple solution would be disappointing indeed.

It's a mistake to suggest to a young business executive who tells you he's "overworked," that he might try organizing his time.

All you have to do in order to sidestep the embarrassment of trying to be helpful on such imaginary problems is to remember that there are a great many people who rave about being in "jams" merely for the purpose of impressing others with their popularity or their social or business activities. They have no real problem, but they wish they had and they do their best to cook one up because they think it's the hallmark of an important person. The safe thing to say in all such instances is, "My, oh my! I don't see how you do it!" Or, if you're not allotted enough time to say all this, just listen attentively and say, "My, oh my!"

Now let's get down to the definition of some real problems.

When it comes to defining real problems, the main pitfall to look out for is this: *We are inclined to take the*

THE REAL PROBLEM AND POSSIBLE SOLUTIONS

*first possible solution that happens to pop into our minds,
and make the mistake of thinking that's our problem.*
The result is that we sometimes overlook the real problem and do not give ourselves a chance to consider *all
possible solutions.*

Nearly every detective story has its dumb flatfoot
who is carried away with some first possible solution and
who wants to make an immediate arrest. But it also has
the seasoned detective who uses his powers of observation and then constructs several different ways in which
the crime could have been committed, examines the
various possible solutions, and finally, by the process of
elimination, arrives at the correct conclusion.

WHAT A NURSE DID

A short circuit in an x-ray machine sent 75,000 volts
through the body of a technician in a leading New
York hospital while he was taking x-ray pictures of a
patient.

The nurse on duty became panicky when she saw the
technician collapse, his hands still gripping the wired
plates.

The first possible solution to this problem which
flashed through her head was wrong. She made two attempts to pull the technician from the high-voltage machine. Each time blue flames shot out and she was hurled
across the room.

Her screams attracted the attention of an attendant, who immediately sensed the real problem.

He turned off the current. And saved the technician's life.

This attendant dealt with the real problem while the nurse mistook the first possible solution that came to her mind for the problem itself. To her, the problem was to free the technician from the wired plates, whereas the real problem was to stop the flow of electricity.

WHAT A GREAT MID-WESTERN DAILY PROPOSED

A newspaper column in a great Mid-Western daily proposed the following question to the public: "Do you think all autos should be condemned when they reach a certain age?" The public argued back and forth on this question, overlooking the fact that the real problem is that of promoting safety, and that condemning automobiles at a certain age is merely one possible solution of the main problem and not a very good one at that. Obviously, more adequate possible solutions would be periodic tests of all automobiles, irrespective of their age, and even more important than this, adequate tests for drivers, as in this particular state it is still unnecessary to pass any kind of driver's test before operating an automobile.

WHAT A WOMEN'S CLUB PRESIDENT SAID

WHAT A WOMEN'S CLUB PRESIDENT SAID

The newly elected president of a women's club told me her troubles. "Now that I'm elected," she explained, "I find that this club is in a mess. The chairman of our speakers' committee tells me our main problem is to raise some money so that we can get some good speakers or our club will go to pot.

"The chairman of our book-review committee says she needs money for books or she can't function.

"The chairmen of our entertainment and refreshment committees tell me that we've got to boost the dues so that we can serve good eats at our meetings or very few will attend.

"It looks to me as though my problem is to raise some money somehow or else I'll have to fire these committee chairmen and try to appoint some who are willing to work with the money we have. Otherwise, the whole club will fall apart."

"Your club," I told her, "reminds me of a textile mill over in Philadelphia that was in the hands of receivers. I was supposed to get suggestions from the various executives concerning what should be done.

"When I asked the production manager what problems the company was facing, he talked about nothing but machinery, explaining that the real problem was to

73

raise enough money to replace their antiquated equipment with some new machinery.

"The advertising manager told me that the real problem was to raise some money for an honest-to-goodness advertising campaign.

"The sales manager contended that all would be well if the company spent a little money to build up a sales force, enabling them to sell their products direct to the retailer rather than through jobbers.

"Now, obviously, each of these men was talking from his own egocentric point of view. None seemed able to view the business as a whole—to see the total situation. It was not until I talked with a banker, who was holding the bag, that I secured a definition of the real problem. As he put it, 'The real problem is—should this business be discontinued or not? Is this plant, together with its personnel, equipped to make a product that people want and at a price that will permit a decent profit?'

"Now coming back to your club, it looks to me as though you and your committee chairmen have been doing a lot of egocentric thinking, but have overlooked the real problem. Let's look at the total situation—that is, the club as a whole. Unless the club can find some real reason for existence, there's really no reason for its continuing at all. So the real problem is for the club to find a purpose. What is the fundamental purpose of your club?"

"Oh, it's supposed to be a club for the betterment of the community."

"Yes, but specifically what does the club do for the betterment of the community?"

"You know," she exclaimed, "I think you've hit it. Our club hasn't been doing anything really worth while for the betterment of anyone but ourselves. We've been fooling around with a great many small purposes that have to do with our own entertainment and diversion— speeches, bridge, book reviews, topics of the day, and refreshments. What we should do is concentrate on a major purpose each year for the betterment of the community. There are plenty of things the club could do. We could study how our school system might be improved, or how to get rid of the slot machines in the candy stores where our children spend their lunch money, or how to organize after-school activities of our children, or how to look after the food or clothing or hospital needs of deserving charity cases in the community."

And that's the way the new president of that women's club got new life into the club without raising the dues or without firing any committee chairmen. She found something for the club to do which all could believe in and support.

Anyone who takes the time to look at the total situation has a far better chance of defining the real problem and considering all possible solutions.

How to Test the Statement of a Problem

The next time anyone comes to you with his statement of a problem, there are two important questions that you should ask yourself:

(1) Is this statement of the problem based merely on a general observation, or is it based on a precise and analytical observation from the standpoint of what, when, where, and who?

(2) If it is based on a precise observation, has this person stated the underlying problem, or has he merely stated one possible solution?

In everyday business practice you can depend on it that most of the problems which come to you from others will be stated merely on the basis of some general observation which may or may not be sound. It is important to bear in mind, therefore, that in most cases your first step is to test the general observation on which the problem is based by applying the rules for precise observation, before making any attempt to state the real problem.

TESTING A SALES MANAGER'S STATEMENT

Most problems are proposed to us in the same general form as the following, which was brought to the attention of Spencer, the auditor of a large oil-well-supply house.

One morning the sales manager, Warren, burst into Spencer's office, saying, "Sales are way off on our piston rods and we've got to do something about it. Sharpen up your pencil and figure out the lowest possible price that we can sell them at."

After Warren had left the office, Spencer noted that his statement of the problem was based merely on a general observation that piston-rod sales were off. So that Spencer's first job was to examine this observation from the standpoint of what, when, where, and who. For not until he did this would he be in position to state the real problem involved.

Knowing (1) that their rods could be used only in their own pumps, and (2) that there were certain competing rods on the market that could be used in their pumps, Spencer decided to check up in the field and find out why sales were off. It may be that competing rods were displacing theirs in their own pumps. The only other explanation would be that their entire pumps were being displaced by competing pumps.

In his check-up in the field, Spencer did not find a single case in which competing rods were being used in their pumps. Nor did he find any complaints about the price of their rods. Seven companies in three different territories, however, were gradually changing over to competing pumps, and this had apparently been going on for about six months, all of which tied in with the period of decline in sales.

Spencer now knew the what, when, where, and who; he had turned the general observation into a precise one, and was in position to state the underlying problem.

The real problem, of course, was to sell more pumps. To reduce the price of their piston rods was not even a possible solution to the underlying problem. In fact, to reduce the price on the rods, as suggested by Warren, would be just like throwing so much money "right out the window."

Controversial Attitude vs. Experimental Attitude

Once we arrive at the statement of the real problem and list all possible solutions that suggest themselves, it is easy enough to classify these solutions and to select the most promising solutions for further examination, providing we assume an open-minded experimental attitude. On the other hand, a controversial attitude causes us to kill off solutions which might later prove to be of some aid, and it is important not to restrict unduly our possible solutions at this stage in the thought process. Because some possible solutions involve work, if we are to explore them further, they are often rejected by those who are impatient to arrive at a final solution to the problem. Thus some possible solutions are arbitrarily rejected without a sufficient hearing.

In business meetings, all of us have observed possible solutions to problems being thrown out because of the preconceptions of certain members of the organization.

For example, a direct-mail campaign was suggested as one possible solution to a pencil manufacturer's advertising problem. Immediately one of the executives rejected that solution, saying: "Oh, that direct-mail stuff is out. It gets to a fellow's desk, and off it goes into the wastebasket."

Another solution was suggested—"the use of trade publications." Another executive immediately contended that "this trade paper stuff is a lot of baloney."

In other words, both took the controversial approach to possible solutions, instead of assuming the experimental attitude, trying out the possible solutions on a small trial basis and measuring their results on the basis of definite returns per dollar expended. The experimental attitude leads to the gathering of vital evidence and helps us to protect ourselves against the arbitrary rejection of possible solutions on the basis of preconception or prejudice.

Briefly, then, cultivate the experimental attitude—giving each possible solution a fair trial before you assume that it is worthless.

CONTINUING THE CASE OF
JOHN A. MANUFACTURER

As soon as John A. discovered from his field check that housewives praised the competing product because it "gives more suds," "works faster," and "goes farther," he jumped to the conclusion that he would have to either duplicate or improve upon this competing product. He secured samples of the competing product and turned them over to his chemistry laboratory with instructions to find out what was in the product and to develop a soap chip that is "either as good as, or superior to, the competing product."

The chemist went to work, but encountered difficulties.

Meanwhile, sales kept declining in the Chicago territory, and during the course of a long series of meetings about the whole matter between the chemistry department and the sales department, both sides got sorer and sorer.

At this stage, John A.'s attention was called to the fact that, after all, he was dealing, not with the main problem, but with merely one possible solution to his problem, and that there were other possible solutions that should be considered and that would suggest themselves once the fundamental problem was stated.

John A. was willing to listen to any kind of a new

approach. First of all, his fundamental problem was stated as follows:

"How can we get around this troublesome competition of a small sectional competitor in the Chicago territory?"

Then the possible solutions to that problem were listed:

1. Maybe we can make a superior product.
2. Maybe we can fight him by cutting prices, or loading advertising and selling efforts in the Chicago territory.
3. Considering the sectional nature of the competitor, maybe we ought to buy him out.

Not until this was done did John A. fully realize that he had been looking at only one solution, that he had been wrongly considering that solution to be his main problem, and that he had, therefore, been blinding himself to any other possibilities.

In the next chapter we shall see how John A. secured evidence on the possible solutions to his real problem.

The foregoing discussion should be sufficient to show how easy it is for us (1) to jump over the definition of our real problem, (2) to mistake a possible solution for our real problem, and (3) to overlook many possible solutions to our problem because we make no systematic attempt to list them with the total situation in mind or to fairly consider all possible solutions with an experimental attitude.

The basic rules for defining the real problem and considering possible solutions may be summarized as follows:

Rules for Defining the Real Problem and Considering Possible Solutions

Rule 3. Construct a precise and analytical definition of the real problem, from the standpoint of what, when, where, and who.

Rule 4. Keeping the total situation in mind, list all possible solutions that suggest themselves.

Rule 5. Classify these solutions in order of preference.

Rule 6. Select the most promising solutions for further examination.

CHAPTER SIX

Securing Evidence on Possible Solutions

NO MATTER HOW CARE-
fully we define our
problem and consider
possible solutions, if
the collection of evi-
dence on possible solu-
tions is biased, our
conclusion will merely
represent the product
of a prejudiced mind.

Many of our every-
day problems, of
course, do not permit
the time for, or are not

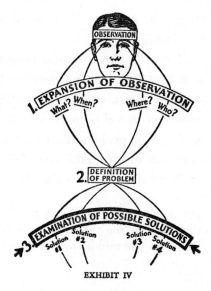

EXHIBIT IV

of sufficient importance to justify, any extended pursuit
of evidence.

But no matter how little or how much evidence we
gather on any problem, we will find that we have certain
opinions and prejudices that interfere with our impartial
reception of that evidence.

Goethe has said, "I can promise to be sincere, but I
cannot promise to be impartial."

How we all eagerly welcome with open arms any kind of evidence that affirms our pet solution to a problem or that agrees with opinions we have openly expressed. And how blind we are to evidence that contradicts our preconceptions. Or, if some one makes himself disagreeable by calling such unwelcome evidence to our attention, how antagonistic and inhospitable we are in our reception.

However, these natural tendencies can to a great extent be tempered and corrected. While it is true that none of us can ever hope to attain that perfect state in which we are able to view evidence impartially on any question or problem that confronts us, yet we can go a long way toward achieving impartiality on any *specific* problem if we make a sincere attempt to—

(1) acquire the capacity to see all sides of a question
(2) appraise the validity of our evidence
(3) keep our minds free from any desire to prove a case

Seeing all Sides of a Question

One evening I boarded the train for home, and buried myself in the newspaper. I don't know how long I'd been riding when I glanced up from the paper and saw from the window that the train was passing some unfamiliar-looking buildings.

"Well, I'll be——! On the wrong train!" I exclaimed to myself.

Jumping to my feet, my first impulse was to get off that train. I didn't know where I was going. I had visions of winding up away out in the sticks, where it would take me an hour or more to get back on the right track. I glanced up and down the car, looking for a trainman who could tell me where we were going and what the next stop was.

I didn't see any. Then, looking out the windows again, I happened to glance out the *other side* of the train. And what do you think? The thrill that comes once in a life-time—I saw some very familiar-looking buildings that told me I was on the right train, after all.

It took me a little while to figure out how this all happened. As I thought back over my daily train rides to and from New York, I realized that for some reason or other I had formed the habit of riding on the *left* side of the car going into New York in the morning, and on the *right* side of the car coming out at night. So that I was always looking at that route from the same side of the train.

I had been doing this day in and day out for months. But this particular afternoon I sat on the *left* side of the car coming *out* from New York. So that when I glanced up from the paper and saw those strange buildings outside the window, immediately the thought flashed through my mind that I was on the wrong train.

This experience really illustrates what habit does for us and what happens to our minds when we form the habit of looking at things from a one-sided point of view. The "other" side of the question or the problem or the situation becomes so foreign to us that we are unable to see that it has any connection with our own. My "train" illustration is so simple that you may find it difficult to believe that such a thing could happen, until you somehow succeed in getting shocked yourself by observing a question or a problem from the opposite point of view. In spite of all our talk about broad-mindedness and the ability to see all sides of a question, it is an unusual achievement for anyone to be able to do so on any question in which his own interests or experiences are involved. It is so unusual, in fact, that it is at first shocking to the one who achieves it.

If you don't think so, try riding on the *other* side of the train or sleeping on the *other* side of the bed.

Or if you want to find out what a familiar street looks like, walk down the other side, or if you want to get a fresh view of your dining-room, sit on the other side of the table. And see what happens.

If you want to get a new view of the business you're working for, try getting the boss's point of view. Or if you are the boss, try looking at it from the employee's slant. If you are trying to sell something, look at the product from the buyer's point of view.

Appraising Evidence

In appraising evidence, consider its source.

Day in and day out we are exposed to all kinds of biased information—sales talks, political propaganda, suggestions from friends and associates who have their own personal interests, yes, even the counsel of members of our own family who have an ax to grind.

We absorb a lot of biased information subconsciously. And we use this evidence in making decisions on a wide variety of problems.

Our democratic form of government is based on the assumption that the individual can think straight for himself and vote intelligently. Yet you know what happens before any election. We are swamped and confused with the special pleadings of candidates. The only information that most of us get as the basis for our vote is so saturated with prejudice and emotion that it smells to high heaven.

In one community a citizens' committee has just been appointed to gather facts about candidates for local office. Just facts. No opinions. Everyone is urged to view the facts and vote as *he* thinks best.

This is a step in the right direction. It helps the voter to think for himself and to base his thinking on a solid foundation. The idea deserves wider application to protect the foundations of our democracy. Freedom has always been taken away from people who can't think for themselves.

Once every four years we get all steamed up over a fight between the Republican and Democratic parties, and are told that the problem in government is to get the right kind of leadership, while it is obvious that it is impossible to have the right kind of leadership in a democracy until the individuals in that democracy are able to think for themselves. You often hear the statement that people deserve the kind of government they get, and that usually refers to bad government. As a matter of fact, they not only *deserve* the kind of government they get, but they *insist* upon it, and they will continue to insist upon it so long as they can be herded and fanned to fury by an emotional appeal which doesn't make sense.

If you were riding the Texas plains and saw a herd of steers stampeded into an emotional frenzy and headed for danger, it would be unwise for you to stand in front of them and try to stop them. History has shown that the "right kind of leadership" has been ridden down time and time again because the people whom they were trying to lead hadn't enough sense to follow that kind of leadership. After World War I, Wilson tried to lead the world to lasting peace. Look what happened to him. Over 1,900 years ago Christ offered the leadership of human brotherhood. Look what happened to him.

Our jury system is based on the assumption that you

can take a scoop out of our population anywhere, and find twelve men or women who are able to separate fact from opinion, weigh evidence, and arrive at sound conclusions. Yet William Moulton Marston, relating in *Esquire* his experiments with juries, points out that even eyewitnesses cannot be relied upon to tell "the truth, the whole truth, and nothing but the truth," and that jurors are typically carried away with the reckless opinions and emotional statements of positive witnesses. In one case, jurors ignored the facts presented by eleven cautious, careful witnesses, and were swept off their feet by one who indulged in a reckless display of opinion and emotion.

Blackstone's definition of a jury is that "A jury consists of twelve men chosen to decide who has the better lawyer."

It's a good system—for lawyers.

It should be. They invented it.

If we are to continue to draw our juries from the rank and file of our population, doesn't it necessarily follow that this rank and file should be told the facts of life on orderly thinking? And shouldn't they be spared the dramatic trickery of lawyers who are bent on proving a case rather than revealing the truth?

"What our friends think" influences us more than we realize. We like to live the life and stay in the rôle which others expect of us. I know a recent graduate from medical school who is now making all kinds of unreasonable attempts to stick to medicine, even though he "hates the stuff," merely because he insists on playing the part which is expected of him by relatives and friends.

How many times is flattery used by so-called friends who would influence us to do something that is to their advantage but not to our own? How many times do parents dominate the lives of their children long after they are three times seven and married?

Wives have a way of interfering with a man's pursuit of his work, especially if it makes undue demands on his time, or involves a change of location, or if it does not measure up to the growing social prestige of the family.

A young woman, recently married, was discouraged by her husband from continuing her studies in music. The husband contended "you haven't got a voice." But the wife is sure that what is really in the back of his mind is a fear that she might become too independent if she trains herself for the teaching of voice, and furthermore, he doesn't want to spend the money for the lessons.

Sometimes sweethearts interfere. I know a young man who decided against going to South America for an oil company—even though he wanted to take the job—because his fiancée wanted him to "settle down and get a good job in Pittsburgh." But he hasn't got a good job yet.

It isn't a pleasant thought, but it is none the less true,

that some of the worst advice often springs from the short-sighted and selfish interests of those whom we love most.

Therefore, in collecting evidence on the possible solutions to your own personal problems, don't rely solely on evidence supplied by friends and members of your family who have their own ax to grind and whose opinions, after all, *may* be next to worthless.

As we all know, there appears to be a great willingness in business among individuals and organizations with something to sell, to supply prospects with information on all kinds of subjects. These sellers of service or merchandise often dignify their findings with the name "research." But a critical examination of their work often reveals that they have retouched details, bended dates, and fitted incidents to serve their own preconceived purposes. Then, too, they are likely to report only that side of the picture which happens to be favorable to their own interests.

I do not mean to say that it is impossible for truth to originate with a person whose interests are involved. For often some of the most significant facts on a problem may come from such a source.

Buyers particularly should bear in mind that it is altogether possible for worth-while ideas or useful bits of evidence to originate with salesmen who call on them. It is so easy for a buyer to develop the habit of defending himself against the assault of all new ideas offered by salesmen. Because he is forced to listen to so many salesmen who blindly present their cases from their own egocentric point of view, with no apparent attempt to begin with the buyer's problem, it is not surprising that the buyer tends to acquire a "No" attitude, and to develop an air-tight defense against anything that salesmen may offer.

But sometimes a salesman, in his attempt to get an order, gives birth to a constructive idea or gathers some evidence that is significant and usable. The intelligent buyer, therefore, keeps his mind open to suggestion so as to be able to sift what is valuable from the mass of rubbish and make profitable use of it.

On the other hand, information from so-called disinterested sources cannot be accepted blindly without question, for a well-meaning person, with no ax whatsoever to grind, is not necessarily a skilled observer.

In receiving evidence that involves masses of data, it is well to remember that the "argument of numbers" is sometimes as false as it is old. "Fifty million Frenchmen can't be wrong" is passed off as a joke, but we too quickly believe evidence to be dependable simply because it is backed up with large numbers.

Having a great deal of evidence on a subject does not necessarily mean that this evidence will hold water, that it is secured in a sound way from reliable sources, that it is incontrovertible.

For example, a market study was conducted in which

thousands of retailers were asked to give the selling rank of an individual branded product, that is, to classify it as first, second, third, or fourth.

The results, even though based on a large number of interviews, were misleading. For in most instances retailers, handling hundreds of different products, actually don't know offhand what the rank of a given product is. Nevertheless, they *will answer* such a question. There are many cases in which a dealer's guess has been compared with his actual orders and inventories, and the evidence has repeatedly shown that he all too frequently gives unreliable information when asked to give the sales rank of an individual product.

Here is another interesting case that shows the danger of accepting answers as facts. A survey was conducted in which the housewife was asked if she had bought a given product recently, to which she answered,

"Oh yes. I have a box in the kitchen now. I bought it yesterday."

The skilled interviewer knew that before he could accept this "answer" as a fact it would be necessary for him to actually *see* the box. So he began to talk about the condition in which the package reached her. He told her that the goods leave the factory in good condition, but that he was always interested in knowing how they reached the consumer. The housewife went back to the kitchen to get the box and came back with *another* brand in her hand, saying:

"Oh, say, this is 'Y' brand that I bought yesterday. You know there are so many different kinds on the market, and . . ."

The woman's first answer to the did-you-buy question was "Yes," but the fact was that she *had not bought.*

Briefly, then, evidence must be incontrovertible not only from the standpoint of the *source* of the information, but also the *means* for getting it, before it can be safely used as a basis for any conclusion.

Seek Evidence from Authoritative Sources

No matter what your problem is, it is usually possible to collect unbiased evidence on all possible solutions from authoritative sources.

If you feel the need of personal counsel, it is wise to go to some authority who has no personal interest in your decision.

In the business or professional field, there is not only a vast number of printed sources, but evidence may originate from one or more of a wide variety of original sources—sources within the company, such as technical laboratories, the factory, the company records, and "unrecorded specifics" in the minds of employees all the way from the president to the office boy; sources in the distributive system and in the market such as consumers, retailers, jobbers; sources among "outside" organizations such as government bureaus, trade associations, banks, investment companies, publishing companies, foundations, and even competitors.

Experimenting in the technical laboratory, securing information from human beings within or without one's own organization, analyzing statistics, or appraising the values of evidence from various sources, is no job for an amateur. Neither can dependable information be expected even from a skilled person with special interests to defend or promote.

Whenever the problem at hand is of sufficient importance to justify a well-rounded search for evidence, therefore, it is wise to delegate the job of gathering evidence to a disinterested person who is skilled in the technique of securing the type of evidence desired. Then one can be reasonably certain that the evidence is dependable.

Desire to Prove a Case vs. Intelligent Ignorance

We may *begin* our search for evidence free from any desire to prove a case, but we are in danger of becoming so enthusiastic about some bit of information secured early in our study, that we think we have hit upon the final solution and then we try to prove it. Unless we are constantly on our guard, we will find ourselves jumping to extravagant conclusions from limited facts, even though we have a sincere desire to pursue evidence impartially.

The early reception and pursuit of evidence is certainly the "enthusiastic age" in an orderly thought process. At this stage your impulse is to tell others about your "new discoveries" and even go so far as to write letters or reports about what you have found out. But to do this is dangerous, whether your thinking is along the right trail or along a false trail.

Even if you are on the right trail, it is a mistake to spend your enthusiasm in telling others about your early thinking, for in doing so you dissipate energy that could be used in pursuing your evidence further. And you expose yourself to discouraging objections by critics—objections which you will probably be unable to answer because you have not pursued your evidence far enough.

If your early thinking is along a false trail and you go on record either in conversation or in writing, you lay yourself open to the temptation and the desire to prove the false solution that you have expressed and to blind yourself to other possible solutions.

Those in the medical sciences know how dangerous it is to become too enthusiastic over a possible solution in the early stages of their investigations. For example, a medical researcher in seeking serums or conditions which provide immunity to a certain disease, finds that many black tribes are completely immune, and he feels that he may have hit upon the solution to his problem. But as he presses his case further, he discovers several instances in which the disease is raging among black peoples in certain remote locations, all of which rejects that solution.

Those who are fond of detective stories know how many "false starts" are usually made by the professional detective before he hits upon the trail that solves the mystery and how carefully he avoids any definite commitments until he has thoroughly searched for all available evidence on each possible solution.

"Yes," you say, "but as a practical matter in everyday business, aren't we forced to arrive at decisions on the basis of very little evidence?"

And I agree.

There is no objection to arriving at a decision at any stage during the reception or pursuit of evidence, providing a decision is necessary for action. Our main difficulty is not that we make decisions, but that we permit others to draw us into opinions and decisions *before* we have to make them—that is before we have any occasion at all to act upon them.

And that's dangerous. It's dangerous for the simple reason that once we permit ourselves to draw a conclusion and express it to some one else, we run the danger of crystallizing our opinion on the matter and later, when we have some real occasion for acting, we are likely to support the premature conclusion that we made and to blind ourselves to contrary evidence that has come up in the meantime.

The next time a business associate asks your opinion

on a question, on which little evidence is available, you might first of all raise the question of whether it is necessary to arrive at a decision at that time or whether your associate is merely asking your opinion in order to make conversation. If it is not necessary to arrive at any decision or to take any action at the time, it is best to tell your associate that you prefer to reserve any opinions or decisions in the matter until it becomes necessary to act one way or the other. For meanwhile, further evidence may come to light that would change your feeling about the whole matter. If the other person still presses you, you might say that if you *had* to arrive at a decision immediately, because some action had to be taken without delay, your decision would be so-and-so, it being understood, of course, that you reserve the right to change that decision at any time in light of further evidence.

It is important to recognize that business problems involving human behavior are dynamic, which means that we are, in a sense, forever engaged in the reception or pursuit of evidence no matter what the problem may be.

Our minds should never get "set" on any question. We should always be sufficiently open-minded to review any new evidence that has come into the picture since we reached our last decision and to change the decision if the new evidence points that way.

But unless we make a conscious effort to do so, we will not be open-minded. We will continually go back to our previous decision reached some time ago, and stick to that in the face of all opposition. That's the reason why "experienced" men in any field of business *can* be the most dangerous.

True, we must from time to time arrive at decisions when action becomes necessary. The only thing to remember is that any decision is based on the picture up to that time, and that the mind should be kept hospitable to any further information which may come to light later, and there should be no defense of previous decisions, but rather a willingness to reverse oneself at any time whenever additional information dictates the change.

To keep our mind hospitable to new evidence is to maintain an "intelligent ignorance." For a man simply to say "I don't know" in answer to a question merely demonstrates ignorance. But if he adds to this confession the statement, "Before I can venture any intelligent answer to that question I would have to see some evidence from the standpoint of what, when, where, and who," then you know that that man has sufficient intelligence to know *what kinds of information* he needs in order to arrive at a better-informed decision. This is what is meant by "intelligent ignorance." And it's rare.

John A.'s Case

Now let us pick up John A.'s case again and carry it through the reception and pursuit of evidence.

In this case, the evidence secured by the Chemistry Department revealed that it would involve some long and tedious experiments to uncover the secret process by which the competing product was made. After considerable work, this department was unable to duplicate the product, let alone improve upon it, so that the possible solution of creating a superior product did not prove to be very promising.

Nevertheless, the possible solution of buying the competitor out was not a popular one among the more conservative members of the executive staff, who contended that it had always been the "policy" of the John A. company to overcome obstacles by "fighting" and to grow by "natural means" through hard work, rather than by any such easy course as buying a competitor out. But while these more conservative members talked "policy" and "sentiment," the president's right-hand man gathered some evidence and made some estimates. He estimated that John A. was losing an annual sales volume of about one-half million dollars in the Chicago territory and that this involved a loss in net profits of about $5,500 a month.

Then the competitor was approached through a third party and was asked how much his business was worth— plant, machinery, product, trademark, and all. After studying for several weeks, the competitor reported that his business was worth at least one million dollars, but that he didn't know whether he would sell for that. The negotiator brought back word to John A. that he believed the business could not be bought for less than $1,200,000.

To fight the competitor by cutting prices or loading advertising and selling efforts in the Chicago territory seemed the least promising solution of all, in light of the fact that the competing product was a superior one.

In the next chapter we shall see how John A. weighed his evidence and arrived at his conclusion concerning what action should be taken.

Rules for Securing Evidence on Possible Solutions

Following is a statement of the rules for securing evidence on possible solutions, all of which should be self-explanatory in light of the previous discussion.

Rule 7. Expose yourself to sources of evidence on all sides of the question, rather than confine yourself to sources that give evidence only on one side.

Rule 8. Appraise the validity of your evidence from the standpoint of its source and the means used for gathering it.

Rule 9. Guard against the formation of opinions or premature judgments while in the process of examining evidence.

Rule 10. Keep the mind open and hospitable to new evidence on any side of the question.

CHAPTER SEVEN

Drawing Conclusions

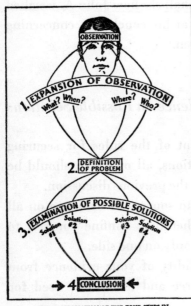

A VISUAL APPLICATION OF THE FOUR STEPS IN
STRAIGHT THINKING

EXHIBIT V

ANYONE WHO KNOWS how to make a decision saves himself a lot of mental torture. Life presents a perpetual stream of problems, each of which demands a decision. Yet so many of the questions with which we concern ourselves, permitting them to upset us and to ruin our dispositions for several hours, sometimes for the whole day, are really of small consequence. The trouble is that we don't seem to be able to realize it at the time.

You know the woman who worries all day about whether she ought to bake the fish or broil the fish for the evening meal. Can't make up her mind until the last minute. Then all through the meal she's wondering whether she ought to finish the ironing that night or get at some of the mending that's piled up. When her husband suggests they go to the movies, she can't decide whether she wants to go to the Strand or to the Palace. When her husband makes up her mind for her by saying, "Let's go to the Strand," she can't decide whether she should just wear what she's got on or put on her gray suit.

You know men, too, who don't know how to make up their minds. They never get far, no matter what they work at. They need someone to make their decisions for them and that someone is usually the boss. Or the wife.

In every home, in every business, in every social group, wherever people gather together, someone has to make the decisions and that someone is the leader, whether recognized as such or not.

If you want to learn how to make up your mind with a maximum of wisdom and a minimum of wear and tear on your mental apparatus, you must learn to distinguish between what's important and what isn't. If a problem is relatively unimportant, you can arrive at a quick decision with the simple assurance that it doesn't make much difference which way your decision falls.

You can develop your own standards. Any expenditure involving less than a certain amount of money can automatically be classified as unimportant.

You can set your own standard in relation to time. As far as I'm concerned, I merely ask myself "What difference will it make one year from now?" If the answer is "no difference," I usually classify the problem at hand as relatively unimportant.

This simple separation of what's important from what isn't will eliminate the petty arguments that make mountains out of molehills at home and abroad. It's far easier to give in to your sweetheart, your boss, your neighbor, or your dog, when you realize that the whole matter doesn't amount to a hill of beans. It will help you if you'll remember that you are no bigger than the things which trouble you.

If, however, the problem at hand is really important, you will want to take as much time as you are allowed, to consider fully the various possible solutions to that problem. On each promising solution, you will want to follow faithfully the scientific rules for drawing conclusions.

Rules for Drawing Conclusions

Rule 11. Set up a balance sheet on each possible solution, stating your evidence for and against that course of action.

Rule 12. Weigh the relative importance of positive and negative evidence in each case, and draw your conclusion in favor of the best course (or courses) of action to be taken.

HOW TO SET UP A BALANCE SHEET
ON AN IMPORTANT PROBLEM

I have never yet seen a case in which no evidence at all was available on which to base a decision. Neither have I seen a case in which all possible evidence was available. Many of the conditions involved in our decision are always unknown. Many not measured. Many immeasurable in any concrete sense. We can never hope to get enough information to give perfect support to all our decisions. But only by bringing to bear on any decision all the evidence we have at hand can we hope to boost our batting average on all of our decisions.

Regardless of how meager or how well-rounded your information on any problem, and no matter how obvious the solution appears to be, it is always safest to set up a balance sheet on each possible solution, stating whatever evidence you have for or against that solution.

A simple way to do this is to draw a line down the center of a blank piece of paper, put your negative evidence on the left-hand side, and your positive evidence on the right-hand side.

There are two important reasons for using a balance sheet. In the first place, it assures that *all* the evidence you have at hand will be brought to bear on your conclusion, rather than only part of it. Without the aid of a balance sheet you will find yourself mentally tormented with all kinds of random thoughts, some favoring a decision one way, others pointing in the opposite direction. Certain bits of evidence will come to your mind again and again, your decision will be swayed one way and then the other, depending on what bit of evidence is in your mind at the time. And after you get mentally sick and tired of the whole business, you will finally reach a decision at the last moment, when you are forced to do so under pressure, and your decision will be dictated by that part of the evidence which happens to be foremost in your mind when you get tired thinking.

In the second place, a balance sheet permits a quick and well-rounded view of advantages and disadvantages. The solution to any problem seldom works out perfectly. There are usually certain advantages that must be sacrificed no matter which way you make your decision. Unless you use a balance sheet, your problem is likely to be left hanging in the air. Your mind will be haunted first by the disadvantages of deciding one way and then by the disadvantages of deciding the other way. In such a mental condition, it is difficult for you to "make up your mind." And there is nothing that exacts such a heavy toll on our mental efficiency as the inability to reach a decision. In fact, inability quickly to balance advantages and disadvantages is what causes most of our mental disturbances and what has been identified by psychologists as the primary cause for suicide.

With the use of a balance sheet, however, you will be able to survey advantages and disadvantages at a glance, reach your decision quickly, and spare yourself the mental torment that comes from excessive deliberation.

An important point to remember in making any decision is that when it comes to human problems, there are no perfect answers. I have never seen any course of action, however wise, that didn't have some disadvantages. On the other hand, it is often necessary to say NO to a great many proposals which have a number of advantages to recommend them. It is a matter of weighing all the known advantages against all the known disadvantages and arriving at a decision in favor of the side with the best score.

It is sometimes said that the world is made up of two kinds of people—the optimists, or positive thinkers, and the pessimists, or negative thinkers.

The optimist or positive thinker is inclined to overemphasize the arguments *in favor* of doing something. He can tell you in detail all the advantages of doing it. But he is inclined to minimize, and in extreme cases, to overlook entirely, all the possible disadvantages.

Shakespeare said that "Love is blind." So is business in many respects. Just as the lover avidly pursues the heroine, blinding himself to the possible disadvantages which may attend the realization of his desires, so it is easy for us in business to become over-enthusiastic about making a bargain or closing a deal, thinking only in terms of the main advantages and blinding ourselves to important disadvantages.

For example, the president of a company faced the problem of securing distribution and consumer sales on a new product. He called on the head of a large chain of drugstores for the purpose of getting the chain to stock it. He was so anxious to make the sale that he agreed to a price that would permit the chain to sell the regular one-dollar package of the product for seventy-two cents. In his enthusiasm he lost sight of the fact that he was making a very important decision. Later he realized that while he had in one transaction secured the distribution of his product through a large chain of stores, yet he had done so at a price that practically ruined his chances of distributing his product through jobbers to retail outlets that control most of his market, but that would have to sell his product for around a dollar in order to make a legitimate profit. If he had made out a balance sheet before arriving at his decision to sell the chain at their price, he might have avoided this expensive mistake.

A paper manufacturer, in his eagerness to secure a large order from a company that wired for a bid, made his cost estimates correctly, but failed to consider the disadvantages of upsetting his production schedule for regular customers. While he secured the special order and made a profit on it, he lost two regular customers during the rush, and it was eighteen months before he was able to get their business back again. The profit sacrificed on this regular business over the eighteen-month period far exceeded what he realized on the big special order.

On the other hand, the pessimist or negative thinker is inclined to over-emphasize the arguments *against* doing something. He can tell you in detail all the disadvantages of doing it. But he is inclined to minimize, and in extreme cases, to overlook entirely, all the possible advantages. For example, I know a woman who can't make up her mind to learn to drive an automobile because she thinks she might have an accident. A barber told me he'd like to open his own shop, but he can't bring himself to the point of doing it, because he's afraid he "might not make a go of it." Another case is that of the woman who wouldn't take a vacation trip because she had a small baby and thought exclusively in terms of the disadvantages of taking it along. Then there's the critic who condemns democracy because it is wasteful and inefficient, but who seems to overlook the advantages of this system. A little later in this chapter, we shall see how John A. Manufacturer's case affords an excellent example of overlooking important advantages.

And so it should be perfectly apparent that, without a balance sheet, either the optimist or the pessimist is in danger of arriving at the wrong conclusion.

When the Evidence Is About Even

In most instances a clear picture of your evidence on a balance sheet makes your decision quite obvious.

However, you will no doubt encounter cases—really important ones—in which one possible solution balances out about the same as another. When this is the case, it probably doesn't make much difference which way you decide on the problem.

A young Negro lover applied for a marriage license at the court-house in a small town in Alabama one warm May morning. About two hours later he was back.

"Say, Boss," he drawled, "ah wants to change de gal's name on dat marriage license."

The clerk was flabbergasted. "Why—you can't do that! What's the trouble?"

"Well, Boss, dere's no trouble, but yo' see, ah just saw anoder colored gal up de street dat ah lak, and ah just wants yo'all to rub out dis name dat ah gave yo'all dis mahnin', and write in dis oder gal's name."

"Why, you can't do that! The only way you can handle a matter of that kind is to cancel the license you took out this morning, and take out a new license. That'll cost you another two dollars."

"Two dollahs?" The Negro pondered a minute. "Well, ah tell yo', sah, jes' let it go, den. Yo' see, sah, dere ain't dat much difference between de two."

There is an old saying to the effect that when you don't know what to do, don't do anything. And this is sound advice, if it is possible to postpone a decision and not do anything. But if you are faced with the problem of reaching a decision one way or the other, and the evidence on two possible solutions balance out about the same, your balance sheets at least provide the assurance that as far as you are able to determine on the basis of your evidence at hand, it doesn't make any difference which way you decide. You can flip a coin and reach a decision one way or the other with the satisfaction that there are apparently as many advantages and as few disadvantages on one solution as on the other.

All this implies, of course, that the evidence on either side of the balance sheet is given the weight it deserves. And although this is necessarily arbitrary in many instances, everyone knows that it is possible to have one point in favor of a decision that overbalances a dozen minor points that may be against it. It is difficult for anyone to tell you the relative importance of the various points that might come up in your consideration of a problem, for balancing positive evidence against negative evidence is largely a matter of good judgment.

But what is good judgment but a product of your mental operations? And if these operations are logical, your judgment will be sound. If illogical, your judgments will be faulty. All kinds of hay-wire decisions can be arrived at, of course, from perfectly sound facts. So that I should say that the statement commonly mouthed, "A man's judgment is no better than his facts," should be changed to read, "A man's judgment is no better than his logical analysis of the facts."

You Don't Always Have to Do One Thing OR the Other

The twelfth, and last, rule for orderly thinking tells us to draw our conclusion in favor of the best course (or courses) of action to be taken. The main reason for a rule like this is that, in weighing two or more solutions to a problem, it is so easy for us to assume that we must do one thing *OR* the other, when very often we can do both.

Recently I had a luncheon date with a friend, Mr. Hudson, who was taking an afternoon train. It so happened that that was the only time he could see me. Along about 10:30 Mr. Thomas, from St. Louis, phoned saying that he was in town for the day and lunchtime was his only available time. It was important for me not only to see both of these men, but to have both as my guests for lunch. In addition, however, I had private matters to discuss with each.

My first thought was that it would be impossible to have luncheon with two men on the same day and yet talk over private matters with each, since each man had only one hour available for lunch.

How would you solve that one without getting yourself into a dither?

The first thing I did was to ask myself, "Is this one of those cases where I *must* do one thing *or* the other, or can I do both?"

112

And out came the answer.

I arranged to meet Thomas at his hotel at 12:15. We discussed our private business until 12:45, when I arranged to have Mr. Hudson come and join us for luncheon. Then, at 1:15, Thomas left for another appointment, and Hudson and I had a private session from 1:15 to 1:45.

A policeman who told me he "would like to study law," added, "but what chance have I got—I've got a full-time job as a cop." He didn't know that there are several policemen who are doing both—holding down full-time jobs on the New York police force and studying law in their spare time.

A sales manager was all snarled up trying to decide whether to pay his salesmen on a commission, drawing account and commission, or salary basis, while a leading competitor of this company was successfully using all three methods.

One of the main reasons why a certain well-known hotel man is so successful with his restaurant business is that he uses four different methods for accomplishing the same objective—a coffee shop, a tearoom, a men's grill, and a main dining-room. Each attracts its own type of trade and all make a nice profit.

The head of a large food-manufacturing business was greatly troubled in attempting to decide whether the company should sell direct to the retailer or through jobbers—until it finally dawned on him that they might do both. Today they sell direct in some territories, through jobbers in other territories, and in some sections they use both methods—selling some types of customers direct and other types through jobbers.

A manufacturer of mill equipment pondered whether he should have his salesmen call on all types of prospects, or whether he should have one group of salesmen cover the textile mills, another group the iron and steel mills, etc. At the same time, a competing manufacturer was using both plans successfully.

True, there are instances in which we waste a lot of time trying to figure out whether we ought to do one thing or another, when we should really do *neither*— when we should go back to the third step in orderly thinking and pick out a new solution. But assuming that we have all the reasonable solutions already in mind, we can safely use any number of good solutions as long as any one of them does not preclude the possibility of following the others as well.

ONLY ONE SOUND MIND IS NEEDED
TO MAKE A SOUND DECISION

Even though a person thinks out a sound course of action, knows what his decision should be and why, he so often lacks the courage to act without the approval and confirmation of someone else.

This is a fundamental weakness that often proves fatal

to action. After all, only one sound mind is needed to arrive at a sound decision.

"Two heads are better than one," is the convenient excuse offered by those who are too lazy to think, or too timid to make up their mind, alone. They can't go ahead with anything unless they get the approval of someone else.

There is no one more colorless than the self-conscious, vacillating person who is neither hot nor cold, wet nor dry, because he is always wondering what others will think of him and is always trying to please everybody.

One thing is certain. You will neither venture anything nor achieve anything if you permit yourself to be unduly influenced by others.

This does not mean that it is impossible to get constructive suggestions from someone else. The most important thing to remember is that you are to use only those suggestions that facilitate a fuller and more accurate expression of the individual objectives which you yourself believe to be worth while.

Man as a group is chaotic. If you follow the changing whims and wishes of others, you too will be chaotic. If, on the other hand, you hold to the thoughts that you yourself know to be sound, you will become placid, strong, independent, sure.

The futile pursuit of the approval of others will distort every worth-while desire in your heart and rob your life of any personal meaning. You can never be really

YOU until you achieve mental freedom from the fears, hates, superstitions, prejudices, and opinions of those on the outside.

Lose that mental freedom and you lose everything.

The attitude of your folks and your friends, like public opinion in the mass, is fickle and contrary. The more you pursue its favor, the less you gain it; the less you yield to it the more it turns toward you. The world intuitively worships a man who has the courage to make decisions for himself.

No matter who you are, if you can only learn how to make up your mind, you will get more done, improve your disposition, protect yourself from nerves, aid your digestion, sleep better at night, and add to your general success and happiness.

Now let us see how John A. Manufacturer arrived at his final conclusion.

Concluding John A.'s Case

As soon as John A. learned that buying out the competitor would involve a cash expenditure of over a million dollars, he said that he couldn't do it. He didn't have the ready money. He would have to borrow it. That meant negotiations with bankers and a lot of work.

It was not until John A.'s right-hand man built up the following balance sheets on two possible solutions that a full picture of the *advantages* of possible Solution No. 2 became clear.

DRAWING CONCLUSIONS

Balance Sheet on Possible Solution No. 1

DEVELOPING PRODUCT EQUAL TO OR SUPERIOR TO COMPETING PRODUCT

Negative

1. Delay for uncertain period.
2. Continued loss of business for uncertain time which involves loss in net profits. Our sales have declined about ½ million dollars a year in Chicago territory—a loss apparently attributable to the competitor's gains. This business involves an estimated *net* loss of $5,500 a month for uncertain time until product has become perfected, has been marketed, and has regained ground lost to competition.
3. While we are experimenting we would continue to lose standing with the trade and with consumers.

Positive

1. The immediate costs involved in developing our own product would be relatively small.

Balance Sheet on Possible Solution No. 2

BUYING OUT COMPETITOR

Negative

1. Immediate cash expenditure of about $1,200,000.

Positive

1. Immediate gain of $5,500 a month net profits on the business now being lost to competitor.
2. Opportunity to make a much larger profit on competing product by selling it nationally through our present organization.
3. Protection from the possibility of similar disastrous competition in other territories if the competitor were to decide to expand his territory.
4. We would avoid expensive battle with competitor.

117

After carefully studying these balance sheets, even the most conservative members of John A.'s executive staff agreed that the best course of action would be to forget about policy and sentiment, go ahead and borrow the money, and save the profits of the business.

And so John A. bought the competitor out, finally closing the deal for $1,150,000.

In the very first year, John A. made a net profit of $300,000 on the new product by extending its sales to other territories through his existing sales force. And the following year the newly acquired product turned out to be John A.'s leader, both in volume and in profits. So that the investment turned out to be an extremely profitable one.

Orderly Thinking Becomes Automatic with Practice

One should not derive the impression that an orderly thought process always involves extended deliberation. For while straight thinking invariably consists of the four main steps that have been analyzed and explained, yet the brain may in some instances perform these four steps in a few seconds. For example, who hasn't jay-walked across a busy street? Your initial observation—that you are on the wrong side of the street, led to the definition of your problem—to cross the street. As you crossed the street, you weighed the evidence of vehicles moving at various speeds, together with your own ability to move to avoid them, and before you reached the other side had arrived at a number of decisions to go in front of this vehicle, then to wait until another had passed, and so on.

The main reason why many people are able to cross a busy thoroughfare so successfully is that they have become highly trained in weighing that kind of evidence and are able to do so automatically. A man from the jungle, who can run faster than you and stop quicker, would be in greater danger of being run down by an automobile than you are, because he is less skilled than you are in judging the speeds of automobiles.

All of us, however, have fallen into faulty habits of thinking on everyday problems, and before we can straighten out our thinking we must carefully analyze the whole process step by step until we at least know how it should be performed correctly. Then it is all a matter of going through the steps correctly often enough until straight thinking becomes automatic. Just as in improving our golf game we must analyze the use of each club, and practice the correct stroke until it becomes firmly fixed in our habit motives, so it is necessary at first to spend considerable time practicing correct thinking step by step.

Right now you are in much the same position as the man who wants to improve his golf game and has taken his first lesson that has to do with the rules for using the driver. In spite of his knowledge of those rules, he steps up to the first tee, takes a healthy swing at the ball in the old way, gets the same old slice, and then says, "Gee! I forgot to hold that left arm straight and follow through."

Similarly, the first time you try to apply these rules for straight thinking, you will probably find that your decision has already been made before you realize it— that you have jumped from observation to conclusion instead of proceeding one step at a time.

What you should do when you find that you have jumped to a conclusion without following the four main steps is obviously to start over and proceed in the organized way. Before long you will have formed the habit of following the four main steps in straight thinking, and sooner than you expect this orderly process will become automatic.

Even after a conclusion is reached on any problem at hand, the mind should be kept open and hospitable to any new evidence that may suggest an exception to, or a future modification of, the conclusion which has been made. For it is only by acquiring a genuine hospitality for new information as it arises, that we can possibly make the most intelligent use of our experience and keep our "conclusions" up to date.

Someone has said that consistency is the vice of little minds. Certainly one important sign of mental greatness is the willingness to change one's mind in the face of new evidence.

Unfortunately, some people look upon it as a sign of weakness for one to change his mind. I know that some executives brag about the fact that once they start a thing, they go through with it. But if you planned a lawn party and it poured rain, it would obviously be unwise to sit out on the lawn in the rain and eat sandwiches. This might sound like a ridiculous example, but how many times have you observed a business man stick to a given plan in spite of "hell and high water" and congratulate himself on his "stick-to-it-iveness."

Now that you are reasonably familiar with the twelve rules for straight thinking, and have seen them applied to a variety of business and personal problems, you are invited to go on with your studies in straight thinking and to read the following books, all published by Harper & Brothers:

1. "How to Find and Follow Your Career," in which the same rules are applied to career problems.
2. "How to Improve Your Human Relations," which presents the four primary mental levels in all human relations, together with a simple mental attitude for opening closed minds which conforms with all the fundamental rules for straight thinking.
3. "The Law of Intelligent Action," which represents the results of the application of the rules for straight thinking to the study of intelligence, and which has been called the most significant law of our environment.

Since democracy is based on the assumption that the masses of people can think for themselves and vote intelligently, we must teach the rules for straight thinking as part of our program of general education. If we have any hope of achieving democracy among many of the other nations of the world, we must teach the rules for straight thinking in many lands, all over the globe. In fact, if we are to learn to live together at home and abroad, if we are to save ourselves from self-destruction, the vast majority of the people in every important country on the face of the earth must learn how to think straight, before it is too late.

This task represents the greatest challenge which every thoughtful person faces in the immediate years ahead. It is our responsibility. It is my responsibility. It is your responsibility.

Summary of Rules

I. RULES FOR MAKING PRECISE OBSERVATIONS

Rule 1. Define the primary facts in connection with your observation, and separate these facts from any opinions or impressions.

Rule 2. Analyze the facts, as far as they will permit, from the standpoint of what, when, where, and who.

II. RULES FOR DEFINING THE REAL PROBLEM
AND CONSIDERING POSSIBLE SOLUTIONS

Rule 3. Construct a precise and analytical definition of the real problem, from the standpoint of what, when, where, and who.

Rule 4. Keeping the total situation in mind, list all possible solutions that suggest themselves.

Rule 5. Classify these solutions in order of preference.

Rule 6. Select the most promising solutions for further examination.

III. RULES FOR SECURING EVIDENCE
ON POSSIBLE SOLUTIONS

Rule 7. Expose yourself to sources of evidence on all sides of the question, rather than confine yourself to sources that give evidence only on one side.

Rule 8. Appraise the validity of your evidence from the standpoint of its source and the means used for gathering it.

Rule 9. Guard against the formation of opinions or premature judgments while in the process of examining evidence.

Rule 10. Keep the mind open and hospitable to new evidence on any side of the question.

IV. RULES FOR DRAWING CONCLUSIONS

Rule 11. Set up a balance sheet on each possible solution, stating your evidence for and against that course of action.

Rule 12. Weigh the relative importance of positive and negative evidence in each case, and draw your conclusion in favor of the best course (or courses) of action to be taken.

What Is the National Institute for Straight Thinking?

SO MANY READERS OF OUR PREVIOUS BOOKS HAVE INQUIRED, "What is the National Institute for Straight Thinking?" that we make the answer to this question part and parcel of this book. The following facts on the background and present work of the institute will help you to understand our purpose.

In the Fall of 1932, Dr. Reilly founded the National Institute for Straight Thinking for the purpose of applying the rules for straight thinking to business and career problems. Since that time, the rules have been successfully applied to a wide variety of other problems as well, and today, the institute offers counsel on business problems, career problems, and problems in the field of general education.

In its business consultations, the institute has been called upon to guide the organization of new business enterprises, and to solve a wide variety of personnel, marketing, production, and organization problems for old and well-established companies.

In its career work, the institute offers a private consultation program on career planning and vocational guidance at the adult level, the college level, and the high-school level.

In connection with this career work, the institute has developed, over a period of years, a series of practical career and vocational tests which reveal a person's basic abilities, and even more important, his personal like and dislike patterns. His basic strengths and weaknesses are measured in relation to his abilities, his desires, and his human relations. High-school and college students are counseled on their immediate educational programs, as well as their longer-range objectives. Adults are counseled on (1) the building of a salable background, (2) the development of personal sponsorship among potential buyers of their services, (3) the improvement of abilities, desires, and human relations, (4) the actual sale of personal services at the right price, and (5) the avocational search for some interest that promises to develop into one's own business beyond the age of 55.

The institute has recently undertaken the task of collaborating with high schools and colleges in the development and installation of courses of study in which the twelve rules for straight thinking are applied to:

1. Career planning and vocational guidance.
2. Problems in human relations.
3. Business problems.

Educators who are interested in initiating or improving courses of study on these subjects, are invited to write the institute for further information concerning teaching materials which we have developed.

The institute work enjoys the sponsorship of many leading executives and educators. Dr. Reilly's books on business and career planning are now used in a number of high schools, colleges, and universities, and he has been engaged by such educational institutions to lecture on these important subjects. The National Broadcasting Company has granted the institute requested time for its "American Family Forum" round-table discussions.

From time to time, the institute holds special educational discussions to which members are permitted to invite their friends.